MW00744057

C l e f

A thirdway
—— *we* ——
—— *key* ——
between "fiction" and "real"

T<small>REATISE UPON THE</small> A<small>UTONOMOUS</small> I<small>NDIGENOUS</small>:
this holy input is not the derivative
of any school but of devotion

j/j hastain & t thilleman

S<small>PUYTEN</small> D<small>UYVIL</small>
New York City

Portions of this text appeared in Skidrow penthouse #15. Grateful acknowledgment is made to the editors, Stephanie Dickinson and Rob Cook, for permission to reprint this text.

copyright © 2013 j/j hastain & t thilleman
ISBN 978-0-923389-08-6

Library of Congress Cataloging-in-Publication Data

Hastain, J/J
  Clef : treatise upon the autonomous indigenous / j/j hastain & t thilleman.
     pages cm
  ISBN 978-0-923389-08-6
  I. Thilleman, Tod. II. Title.
  PS3608.A8614C57 2013
  811'.6--dc23
                              2013021411

This manifesto is for all the gentle
martyrs who have never known
that anyone cared about
them while the storm
rained its blackened
t r o m p e - l' œ i l
    o   *n*
      u   *s*
        a
        l l

Clef Manifesto

Sometimes as they flew the angels fell a bit
before catching themselves again on the night air.
j/j, *"Xems"*

Wriggling in depths of you your
voice   night's dark also knows
tt, *"Shiru"*

We

a bigger entity than can be imagined.

Making music to be
heard, to embody
us
in an infinite experience of subjection,
rejection. Doing so to become

our own god.

Thrusts

contemporary or post-
contemporary (not repeats), this embodying

GOD EVERYWHERE.

We do this because we have to.

As Dharma-rejects we are driven to penetrate

the infinite   eventual

the swallowing of   Energetic

intimations breed this: an unheard of speech

written by angelic

concentrations   follow-throughs.

These Angels Have Sway.

Unconditional investors

because of *incestuous* love for

Angels

prefer each other

.

A
Community of
Correspondence

We were interested in conducting an interview. But what began as a series of rather rote-based interrogations eventually turned toward a philosophical discussion regarding the nature of poetry. Later, after months of corresponding, months of thrashing out positions regarding the art, we both began to realize a defining moment working through us. That moment can best be seen as an examination of literature and art in a community-based awareness (as opposed to a "collective").

The usual commodification of the term *community* makes for not just a bit but an extraordinary amount of suffering. Consuming essential factors of composition the over-use and false application of collectivity preys on the physical heart.

Creative acts are either defined or have a will which had from the first driven their newness, their appeal, toward the idea of *contemporary*.

To be *here* and be of value *here and now* was not just an isolated, individual moment in the creative process, nor was it a method or system-making enterprise. *Here* made itself known to us, through us, as contemporaneity, by way of a passage of *artistic devotion* not always articulated as zeitgeist; more, rather, the geist or gist which would hint at deeper reflexive capacities within the world.

What j/j and tt (who have come together to haunt each other's pages into expansion) became now reads as a meditation which acknowledges that there are currently not enough models for engagement of the ravenous *it*. Ravenous because "now" <u>it</u> is set to consume caverns of overlap, of psyche and the physical, to have focus be on the minute aspects of the whole, to gauge instant by instant the flickering particles that push toward gesture; gesture is itself push re society/ socialization *or* solitude.

There is still need for an ethics proceeding in ways that do not diminish cosmic pursuit (and only an individual body can authentically elaborate what their cosmic pursuit/s are). Knowing this requires the seeker seeking and moving forward into contemporaneity. This requires so much.

The subject is <u>not</u> part of any scene. What we discovered through our letter-writing was that beauty could not be isolated or put into a bag and finalized.

All of the mechanical attributes of the art of poetry (and that included the most intangible, like song or airy musics) were also part of a community of subject-matters whose transmissions share a core experience. That experience is no longer an empirical device meant to colonize outward; rather, there is an inner drive toward the visionary. It is, in short, that vision became part of an in-ness the likes of which demanded a new type of history in order to articulate or call itself forward, to vivify itself by making itself *toward*.

Working with infinity in
order to make it able to be
felt or sensed in/as instant
(in ways that are specific)
became the radiating body
of our correspondence.
In order to find the
type of *eyes* that ensure
elucidation, we found
need for embodying
postures that honed each
other's lyric.

Postures are declarations
and they most certainly
are devotions. Postures
are dual holdings, ways
to provide supportive
alternates to dueling.
Postures stitch together the
otherwise rote/socialized
space of composition.
We took our respective
author's names and turned
them into pages in a poise
to touch one another's
work *everywhere*.

As if we were setting ourselves up to be the first to ever engage the entire page in this way, each day became a kind of *asana* toward prayer, toward the writing surface, then from surface to depth and beyond depth. What is beyond depth?

Instead of focusing letter
and response upon a kind of
civility *only* we allowed each
newest gesture to become
a community of intentions.
This then is the ravenous *it*
becoming an image for an
each other, ready to elucidate
at the edge (the *other* of the
page) and then willingly be
delivered back to the center,
the core of the page (the *other*
as *specified*, as volitioned
spark and fire).

Treating retinas as mingled zones is a way to replace traditional regiments of many kinds.

We were able to recognize in this kind of olden form of communication (arts & letters!) a way to disregard typical or technical aspects of writing, of careerism, of (in other words) thematics as dissociative value. There is no value in dissociating from the eye you reside in and must finally come to rest within in order to see.

Oh how many

layers the synaesthetic of our

writing induces ("between letters

and lines, and all around the blank

margins, the spirit circulates free."

(Kazantzakis, *The Last Temptation*

of Christ)).

We can travel back, or rather <u>in</u>, discovering not only a mere chronology of our relationship to the page, but a presence which may or may not ever find its final word or phrase to be thus enshrined. The point is that meaning has moved into the body <u>not</u> as an isolated individual but as a communal compound of impulse and impetus, of fractal-word on the glowing underbelly of a cryptomaniacal culture. This movement into the body can be thought of as a toggling not bound to only two parts.

Is there a difference between freedom and *feeling* free?

How much emancipation is interior sensation in relation to emancipation, and how much is it something that can be given or taken away by an exterior agency? This is important because the zone of our work is interested in upholding interior experiences of emancipation (not only upholding them, but discovering ways of supporting and nourishing them).

"Though the critical cliché has always been that there

is no new content, content is my experiment now []

I see my experimentalism now in these taboo roots."

SHARON DOUBIAGO

(upon finding out that she is

descended from the Eastern Cherokee)

Opinion/ Position About Making Pages

To open the yawn into a caw or a yelp. A page that is always a simultaneity or a multiplicity, a vision and a statement about the importance of need and embodiment as *activist gesture*. Notating movement from boredom or stasis into activated stance. This must be done in order to show the synaesthesia of upholding and feeding as fully forming the act of giving and receiving. In other words, intending and integrating by way of offer. Stance *is* unconditionally for offer, isn't it?

As simple as stance may seem it is very much overlooked regarding the growth of visionary articulations. How to articulate the vineyard being transplanted into the bottom of a boat for example. How and why?

How to articulate the vineyard being transplanted into the bottom of a boat for example.

When You
Rain
You Pour and
That's Very
Reassuring to
Me

If there's any statement to be made it's the need to reach into your own whole life with and through someone else!

Create and inhabit a place without inhibition, a place where it is possible to meet and never have to tell lies because every story there is held and holds an eggshell that can be overwhelmed and is universally fragile.

So, pieces as
place, then.

Places of radical body-

permission
where no
one has to
withhold.
This means
standing
there with
your hand
outstretched
as a car

continues
approaching
you. The
importance
of staying;
to follow the
summons
through.

On Self and Worship

Self *can* be worshipped.

Worshipping worship (as an oscillating vortex, a vacuum of all curiosity and exercise) is worth it.

Worship of self or of another's selvage (as method for proceeding ethically toward enlightenment) in a venerable manner: is *not* narcissism, is *not* misplaced love (though it require devotionist myopias).

Devotionist myopias can be refining fire for deepening understanding, for removal of chasms and illusions of many types.

Self is undeniably subjective. So are visions.

Dreams and
self are both
subjective, so
are visions.
So, to bring
those three
into worship-
oriented

proximity, to
enable their
overlaps, let's
guarantee
a mixed
zone where
fruition *can*
come.

Selvage
or Selva Oscura

Are you
from the
wilderness
or the city?
Lights and
loams in
the dark.

The hems to any head-scarf were made to reflect the stars. Each and every thread of whatever color or persuasive twist must be allowed to enter the consecrated, the profane grotto. The grotto need be a place that is *inclusive* of wafts of all types. The lowly can be brought high, not because of what position thinks itself as high, but because the light and gold alchemical threads which weave the head's adornment mean to display alternates in *emanation* (now we want to speak about gender).

Who would be vain enough to own one sex/gender identity *over* another? It does happen, of course, in contemporary settings which is something that (as occurrence) alternates can be made for: attention paid to the weave which brings animus, brings syzygy upon the scene. Syzygy (the meeting and entwining of inner identities and even the identities worn in a moment) as opposed to a politic or religion or unconditional stricture of form.

Lost in a wood at the middle of one's age, it is possible to embrace the myriad as if the myriad were your mother. The *largess* of what hangs can be perceived as weighty, meaty assistance. If you reach, you will be enacting a gracious host to your most troubled, darkest renderings. To reach is a way to ensure your stretch toward, even if you are never met by the touch of whom you supposed you were reaching toward.

When you find yourself miraculously *found* in the wood, right on the ohm-ing brink of the fire pine's burning, open all of your niches. The seeds (which prior to that transitional brink, were shut tight inside the cones) need the high temperatures in order to release. Opening your niches while *release* is occurring will enable all that is (accrued in) you, to change.

Morphology and its relation

(change)

(change)

to
experimental
deifications.

The IT
as Sky Burial, or,
a Prism Becomes
You

We renounce the face of relationship as *one face* only. No one face has come to us in this life, but *many faces* do come to us. We no longer work for a cosmopolitan concept which outwardly manifests only one relation as its global content. We pursue a multi-faced manifold. A space of facets.

TO EAT AND BE EATEN.

In order to have the *eat* and the *to be eaten* able to occur simultaneously (as opposed to one after the other) there is need to guarantee that there are things to offer: hand extending to waiting hand with something in it. In order to guarantee that there are things to offer, in this type of simultaneity-based context, there must be *excess.* **ADDITIVE ASPECTS MUST CONTINUALLY BE CREATED.**

Our relation to *things* must be overwhelmed by the entrance of a partaking, a psychic meal. There have to be inner aspects to replace all of these objects. The meal is offered and offers, not stopping at appearance. The Tibetan highland ritual after death is just such a psychic meal: begins with the corpse, which has already retired all that is life. In this regard, it has become a site that itself is no longer of the same quality of meaning as it was when it was inhabited as vehicle and drives to carry meaning forth. **Mental lips don't retire when the physical lips are ravenously removed by vultures.**

From the place of eating and being eaten (as a simultaneity) we can write and speak and talk of sight, of what the eye beholds, no longer within an ocular prison. This is how to milk the piston. This, how a prism becomes you.

Saliences

of a Non-Scene:

an Inebriated List

From and For the Prism

-Find ways to leave the doors wide open *and* feel safe at the same time

-Obsess about
embodying a voice
that has space in it for
the voice of the other/
others

-Slowly sew yourself
a more relevant flag

-Write while naked, sing
while naked, perform on
stages naked

-Paint
with
honey

-If having one relationship
constitutes the totality of
citizenship, then renounce
your citizenship

-No longer
work for a
cosmopolitan
concept which
manifests only
one of us as its
global content

-Play
with your
instrument

-Slant does
not erase
a straight-
edged razor
but becomes
its non-
sublated
vow to all
architectures

-Respect for the intelligence of someone does not then become license *against* that someone

-If
communication
is what is
prized, valued,
traded upon,
then stop
hiding, stop *de-
materializing*

-Hair on a hairbrush arrives by way
of what was an egg

-When eggs start to grow hair on their exteriors you will know you have successfully begun to torque receding

-Suck the crimson petal until
your habitus crimps

-Place belief before your judgment

-Grace before your pate

-Palate or penchant before your politic

-In potent abilities for each other, stay; stay

together before during and after all interpretation

A Person
at a Gate

j/j hastain says of composition:

> "The process involves a sort of divergent divination/haruspex
> (hence the presence of sound and image conjunctions in the
> work (these magical stirring and strumming wands)) working
> *with* the thicknesses of phrases and curvatures, then carving them
> into neoteric shapes by way of a slow whittling (by echolocation/
> reverberation of many types). I would say there is always this
> working with an extant bulk (a moment, a feeling, a memory from
> this plane or from another, a sensation, an idea, a gnawing, a bruise
> that I cannot remember where I got it from, etc.) and whittling
> it to a previously unforeseen specificity that allows some sort of
> crossing to occur. **The point, though, is to get an *it* specified, not
> to make thinness (due to the whittling) out of anything, because
> this work of mystery shares lineage with wishes and a wish is
> never thin or brittle.**"

It is still interesting to note that the cornerstone of Freud's
seminal work, *The Interpretation of Dreams*, manifests its major
elucidation via a subject's "wish-fulfillment." I am not calling j/j's
approach to poetic composition into the defining medico-historical
realm here. Rather, I want you to see that an approach to the
body *is* the materialization of rationales and intuitions the body
was *thought* to harbor. In this same look back as well as forward
the move j/j makes is toward updating, toward moving, defining
the many re-cognitions the body gives out. This measurement is
always true, even if the philosophy, even if the empirical site, veers
toward other subject matter; the genesis of what the body *is* exists
in the movement toward *it*. This is a work ethic and it calls into its
measure many forms of devotion.

Now, this devotion and its practice could manifest a yearning
to raise the body above all other known things, or it could be a

movement over the body, to contain and control that influence. Either way, the impulse to be *toward* the body has already created activation sites for the body and so a singular body is always a memory containing every other memorialization as its activation. Dreams may be cast as part of this memorial site, in other words.

Our task (in composing) is to render *non-static* all the static armatures of trope and language as carriers for semantic and syntactic meaning. This is very elemental.

Yet so much attention is paid to the behavioral aspects of these pages that the composition ceases to have anything but caricature unifying its parts. That is not the way it has to be.

Recognizing composition as an assemblage of parts makes it over into a material among all other materials. All matter works for the parts of composition as long as they remain parts, as long as they are found in the greater diversification of materials that matter truly is. An ecstatic movement rules the parts as opposed to the whole, in other words. You will see that this is true when you realize that correspondence is not an intersection with nations, but peoples; that the meaning of one tiny micro-scope is in mirror to a macro-scope.

This is clearly a call to creativity thoroughly engaged with the body. Matter communicates with all other matter (via the memory of its pre-monitions). Bodies seek a shared space to open themselves for one another in that pre-dawn space.

But are these spaces easy to acquire? The answer is they are not easy, they are hard to come by (whether through building a "proprioceptive cave" or by entertaining the open-and-shut sky of history).

We are most interested in the continuance of (what j/j refers to as *it*) the specificities which can elucidate "bulk." We are involved with a movement that has begun to recognize its stretch toward, then inside, the body.

... he stood before the imposing structure but knew there were elements in its wrought which would trip the hinges and then....

behind him, no time to think, he quickly grabbed one of the baskets that were lined up along the hedge-row walls. He then tossed the clippings over his body as a way of testifying that he was one with the thorns and shavings and the mulch, now beginning to putrefact in the summer heat.

...loud foot-traffic and voices .... were these the conspiracies, were these the conspirators that whispered in the ear upon death?

So the figure is a he, then. Are all *he's* verdigris of some kind? Or at least in states of verdigris? He asked himself this as he recalled refractions of modes: moldy ants. He knew the mulch over him would make him momentarily infinite, might even make him seem *impossible* to onlookers (because of his ongoing presence within severe sound).

Are there times when adding makes a severance? He wanted to temporarily sever their sight.

0000000000

Entering the Yoni Space: On Oneness as Opposed to False Plurality

Unioning:

Union (being made) is what first inspired life into living. Mitochondrial bringing by way of this shared binge.

Once is not

enough.

What we are never rests in

names alone. There is a feeling-

knowledge that does not rest

either. It interacts with us as

friction, as a face and being

encountering

god.

There is a sheet of music to play;

there is an instrument to be played.

To play without being "schooled"

in playing, to play from and with

feeling-knowledge is to engage the

mess and what the mess might reveal.

Mess: that thaumaturgical
anatomy that appears to
and through densities that
are always round. Slinging
neutrinos through excess,
through inferno in order to
alchemically render changed
visibility.

To open seeing in different
ways: more-than retinal ways.

Because of chemistry and physics, we think of biological processes as a way to parse out what we encounter in the mental space. Because of political beliefs we transfer that 'world' into the mental space. We do this for all the other so-called facts.

But when "facts" enter the mental space, they are no longer facts, but fictions, fairy tales, myth. It is our work to generate integration. To have mental processes incline toward the way the brain, heart and mind actually flourishes joy and contentment.

Expression can be an indelible

act of
contentment.

A Person
at a Gate, Say.

He realized that they'd never have time to see him slip up to the rounded rows of petals above the lintel, knock three times and utter the phrase: *she's a mystic, a shaman, a rose tattoo.* The quick lunge of all bodies made him misplace time and space. *And all it took was a natural ...*

...but wait, someone else was afoot. Would he hide this time, mask himself as a servant? Or would he simply...

All it took was a natural between; a masculine rose proceeding. Oh the difference between misplacing and forcing dis. This was a dissection of time into. This was the spinning and spilling forth of duration.

Can the new time have a fixed gender pronoun? Is that even possible?

The new time by intent: gems not shorn of their fuzz. What would the sweet diamond look like with its beard left intact?

The figure bent below the copse-curves, not having entirely disappeared but not staying obviously visible either.

So he did then in the hallway, next to the row of vases and vessels, crouch on his haunches. The sound in the distant halls was suddenly growing fainter, and his heart began to beat, and then recede with the sound itself. Years later he would still be there. The steps having gone away (the steps that made the distant sound he had followed into this keep). Time moved without him and he and the vessels that once were used to fill up and contain became boggy, groggy. This was now an archaeological site, a memory of hands washing in vessels. It was the memory of one witness in particular, sitting alone in a cave or corner of the keep, staring out from stone, staring out from wall, ready to receive the hand that could beam its way toward the eye. His living was a life now taking on the first pulse of being, over and over. Memories of the wood shot through his pose in a beauty beat.

It was surprising to him that a figure from within, below a surface, could be looking *out*. He recognized gaze there as a type of viscera, both haunted and not to be averred. He recalled reading how nomadic wilderness monks do not sleep on their backs with their hands clasped over their hearts because they believe that the souls of everything they have ever killed are stored in the fingerprints on their thumbs. Sometimes he felt smothered by gaze from *within* the wall. Sometimes he wondered if the fact that there was so much within the wall committed him to an outward look. Instigations moved like Oligochaete: peristalting toward possible proliferation.

The damp shades aurealed this place with a strange silence. There was an approximation of two faces hanging or being hung from above, as his own neck. They were there, shooting out like a vowel maneuver, suggesting rising pitch teeming from surroundings. He felt this as a suggestion and a gesture responding to presences swaying above him. At the moment of vacated mouth a blast lifted him in reverse of a vacuum or turbine. A blast of wind set him against the wall, having stripped him or shorn him of some of his fur. As the wind rumbled, then dramatically cut out, the music began to commence in full assembly.

Carding the chords, charting the flickers.

He noticed a warmth on the wall as he was slammed against it. He noticed that it was the same thing he was being blown against, stopping. He viewed that slam (even though temporary and not without physical pain) as a holding. Moving slowly to a fetal position (because he was already on the floor) he pondered where pivot and intuition meet.

Kept saying out loud:

"In droves   the roving doves   within the bronze boy."

From within a vision: burning. Large rows of incense stems, burning. Wafts flooding over and under. Then, a vision of rain that leads to actual material dirt beneath his hands. He has gotten to the bronze boy, which is the *hard-on*, the pressings of the music. It's a white bronze and he has somehow arrived.

The gaze within the wall felt like it was leaking out of the wall and onto him. It was protruding: a type of phantom?

Mirror alloy is known for its capacity to emanate brightness without causing discoloration-confusion. He had no idea that when he felt the gaze move from within the wall, it was preparing to plate him, to cover him in an armor that could never be removed!

When he later found (during the time spent on the floor dreaming) he *had* been plated, he *would* study plating processes vigorously, trying to understand what was meant by the fact that in order for him to have been pursued for the sake of being plated he must have been a conductive surface to begin with.

Standing barefoot now on the cold floor he recited: "Plating is a practice that is done to adorn objects, to inhibit corrosion, to increase solderability, to limit friction, to modify conductivity."

He noticed his hands. They appeared as two sides of an open book: "Thin-film deposition has plated objects as small as an atom, therefore plating finds uses in nanotechnology."

When pronouncing the words about atom-based plating he was suddenly overwhelmed with the feeling that the gaze in which he was engaging was within him, watching him as he tried to engage the new thin plate that surrounded his skin.

It was the inherent advocacy of nano-technological boundaries which made him leap, revealing the inner wall-eye as a species of fish.

The fish began rigorously flopping out of the wall already gutted. He experienced the vision of the fish as a guttural emanation.

Each scale of the now opened and eviscerated species he turned over into a kind of model to be used for proceeding.

He began to make successive leaps, first within the armor-plating, but then from the armor-plating which now had overcome the left side of his face. As tender and soothing as it was to be in the time-shade of non-decomposing and non-yearning eternities, he abruptly turned his attention to the olfactory at the back of his tongue and from there saw arcs in a span of dusk. This visualization invited a chamber to open at his side.

From the hollow chamber that opened at his side, this: the color and feeling of ash. At first he was overwhelmed by this oncoming sensation. He was worried it would spread, injure the open fish. He wondered about the vulnerability of shapes that are partially dead and partially animate. When he leaned down to attempt to stroke the disemboweled, something began to leak from the chamber at his side.

First he fingered the leak, wishing he had a mirror so he could track the qualities of the emission. He looked down into the strewn fish as the drips of the leak fell. What he saw as he looked into the fish felt like his own reflection: himself, one of the genders of gaze.

In that moment what was previously dark moisture on his fingers (from probing the leak in his side) rapidly morphed into triplicating red and white roses.

It was a wave sweeping over an apparition. Could he see through all things? He realized that not seeing through all things had pumped his shape into its *present* animation. This would be his secret; this was his way to stun. The fish would remain with him by remaining within his side.

He picked up some of the fishes, placing them into his imprimatur; an instant turning, a loaf of bread. Focusing on the granules, there were many apparitions and it was indeed a screen he was looking into, but his eyes were grazing over the entire length of the screen. Grazing and gazing, as if for the past 2000 years.

Was everything coming to an end? Is that the singing sign of a real beginning?

He was momentarily frozen in all muscles. Then he found himself in another corridor as if unknowingly.

Jumbled, he pondered: he would need to secure the latches to the place. The key was not on him and he was no longer clothed. This made him shake. "Tremble while ponder," he said out loud. He heard a wild, multi-planar moan spread through-out the castle. The sound and presence of the moan actually pleased him, as if it gave a dimension to his previous fear.

In the new corridor he looked to register the two precise fish in his doughy side. He built a history with them, and built that history in one moment of intent. He knew it: one of the fish ate algae (algae is both animal and plant); the other fish was carnivorous, slowly eating its way out of the inlet in his side: eating its way out by eating its host, bit by sultry bit.

There was a smell that still registered as a depth, even though the incense was used up. The smell faintly reached him, yet also subtly eluded him.

Suddenly he had a whole different set of interests.

Was he pregnant? Impossible, being that he was a man.

He rubbed his face, checking for stubble. A canary yellow light sprang into the corridor.

Was this what it meant to finally be helpless? And what was he helpless to?

He recognized the sensation from the inside out. Helpless. "Helpless to indelible beauty."

He noticed the smell again. It smelled like cherry kringle. It was an obvious smell with obvious associations and that's what made him the most on edge. He longed for something simply unattainable in this place. To eat was absolutely impossible, even if a feast were to suddenly spring from his own body again.

He lay down in the slant of light that sprang forth in the corridor. It reminded him of what the Lamas said in the *Tibetan Book of the Dead*: "A light so bright that you might want to turn away from it, but don't turn. Instead, turn yourself toward it with your eyes completely open."

He situated himself comfortably in the heat of the light, and then in a dramatic performance opened his eyes to the slant.

As he opened his eyes he felt something within him stirring again. He understood that as often as he turned his attention away from the two fish that populated his bread-side, he would be forced by light to return to them.

He curved his arm sharply and tried to implant his whole hand into his own side. When he pulled out the portion that he was able to get into his side, his hand was very red; pigment with rouge petioles, strands adrip.

He kept seeing impressions of the images of a physical feast in the space above his third eye, but every time he extended his hand to try and pick up food, he cringed, chagrined somehow.

However, the images of the feast. The pictures of the feast as they floated there, poised above his forehead, so enticing.

It took him a while, there on the floor in the slant of light, to understand the difference between the physical aspects of the feast, and the images of the feast. Once he was able to tell the difference between these, he reached his stained hand up to his third eye region and extracted an image.

As small as it was, the shape pertained to the repetitive and almost mechanical perception of bread *as*.

How many times had he unpacked the sentence

only to feel that the loaf was a presence in the *world* and not the *womb*.

Joy rolled down his back like a wave of new hair follicles sprouting in the rain. Each hair was a shaft of light penetrating the gloom (behind him): a gloom where he would no longer be found.

He looked down (as a way of looking in) and saw sleeves that were embroidered, a coat belted into place across his waist.

He considered the need to develop an ethics for working with apparitions and signs; a way to regard sentiment semiotically. He knew that his focus would need be in finding a method for maturing while in many places, all at once.

He had considered himself a manifold place, awaiting, but now, with the emergence of the image, he felt so bodily, so informed by form.

Noting himself moving from the chamber he stepped outside of the vault he must have been in and noticed many above-ground graves, surrounding. Each of these graves was covered with overgrown, thorny bramble.

He saw the word bramble in his third eye. Held it there for a moment, before intentionally inverting the word from bramble to bracken.

One expects the water to be wet, but in the instant he looked to his feet, the feet were wading through crinkled reams of yellow paper.

Not paper, leaves whose burnt undersides browned the earth near the sea-shore. Amidst hoof-marks left by man and beast, a distant intonation stapled the air with depth and a metallic clanging language. Machines were taking over the entire hem-line of the mirroring. The leaves were giving way to sand and then marbles. There was a bag, a very large kind of rump-roast-shaped object which he took to be the content-holding entity the marbles had shot forth from.

All of these physical presences were a review for his pledge. Once upon a time he had climbed a garden wall, now he was climbing out of the embodiment of what could only be likened to a memorial vindication of sleep. The shock was as profound as the sea, completely informed of shining glass, absorbing all his aspirations. He let out a gasp.

Understanding his gasp as an outward movement (instead of an inward one), he felt he had somehow become something different than had previously been perceived. Reaching from his vertical stance, he picked up a hand full of marbles.

Their shining glass glistened as he rolled them around, had them crash against each other within his grip so he could hear the sound of smooth fracturing: fracture on a meta scale. He brought the marbles up toward his face. There were sand particles on them, small round dots on the less-small rounds.

He brought the handful of sandy marbles to his other hand, clasping them between both, bringing the mudra of his grip near his own pupils. Then at once, without hesitation, he rubbed the sandy marbles into his open eyes, and he did so with no physical response regarding the contact.

Sleek rendering.

There were two chases going through him. They established him. Each time he thought of the deer with the sling around its ass and the target which was out in front of his face, he named it *non-dogmatic dreaming*.

To take flight was both at once and either-neither, whereby the small grass or sedge he now lie down on, the small tufts buried by the diamond densities of outer space (outer space, that is, as some reality he now seemed to wear like a pantaloon, an ostrich feather, or a bracelet of tweed and silk).

"These are the lights of the sky," he said to himself, and then, as if uttering the only words ever spoken, took up his bag (grown to the size of his palm) blew and popped it by tapping together its round, flattening it, folding it, drilling it into his back pocket. He turned onto his belly to size up the earth. Leaves puffed up in the shape of coins.

"Dear ferns" he exclaimed when he saw them. With a sudden rush of tears he felt in a moment how sizing up was not the right way to be thinking about them *or* approaching them. The coin shaped verdant presences danced against his face, gently tugged at the place where his full beard *should have* been. It was like the plants were stretching to smell him. This made him so soft.

Where had all of his previous seemingly (or socialized) masculine aspects gone? He wondered. He opened his mouth, his eyes, wide. He even tried to open his pores. He wanted there to be more of him that he could offer to them: the little fiddlehead companions.

He hoped they would pour something galactic into him. He hoped he could pick some of them and keep them near him as contour to the bramble that he saw covering the graves.

He knew all of these experiences, the images, the miasma of the recent events, were of much more relevance than what he had previously invested so much of himself into: his *pronoun*.

It wasn't like a sudden shower or even a burst out of the sun's center. More, it was that through the past, pro-nouned, he had somehow melted into *this* night (which was now day) and beheld a garden. Not just any, but *the*.

There was a flavor in the air, green and tough oregano or acacia flowers. The smell seemed to indicate they had been ground into a smoldering elixir which was being passed around through particles in the air. This was not a garden any old former *mister* would have seen coming into view (all those scales having fallen away). This was an *other* sitting on the marge, sitting right there on the verge; no mere reflection, but an *other*. A true companion!

Gulping, stunned.

As if memory had lost its brain (with its pro-nouned former existence.)

They were the occupation of one another, and assumed myriad poses, adjusting this and that from eye-beams and brows to shoulder juts.

Humming victuals from the earthly garden, when asked to recite the alphabet, one was invented, right on the spot! This was an amusing amusement they inhabited, crowding out neither one nor the other.

There was a way in which they grew to know one another. It happened as it had been happening since before the ice ages, presumably (and they remarked about this to one another). They might have missed one another, too, they felt. Had their being apart and their now getting back together, somehow occurred to induce or introduce a familiarity? Had the walls of the castle been something they erected as a monument to one another inside the former pro-noun's expectations?

Their voices seemed to emanate from each other almost

simultaneously. Maybe there was a slight delay but the delay was welcomed for it opened a passage toward one another's company, a home for two or more or even many (windows thrown up into the depths of the garden's demesne-like value). This was the essence, they suddenly both remarked, of the present age. "Deja vu!" they both said. "Jinx!" "I said it first." "No, you were just a tad behind." "Behind? Don't you mean forward?" "Never." "Or always…"

Smiles on teeth like gleaming portents of cellular ability itself.

The one who previously identified as "he" (for the sake of self-reference) felt themselves as different than "him" or "he" when in *this* correlation.

This was recognized as a new feeling; one that, now that it had been felt, would be nearly impossible to give up. Also, the curious sentiment that in the garden (that place of ephemeral *other* aiding this union) might be the only place where it is possible to actually share a pronoun, realizing that bringing the gritty marbles to the retinas is what unveiled the embodiable revelation of one with the other as *together*.

So, as *flagellant*, this one, this now-not-necessarily he, who

used to identify as a he, came to
understand self as not singular,
but in need of another, or others.
Understood that it was required
that certain mortifications of the
flesh be applied with rigor, without
repose or hesitation, in order
to reach and uphold such an
oracular, auric state.

One eye could transpose the
actual eyes of the garden pair.
This was the knowledge of the
body, finally given to each of
them as they moved.

Beyond any gaze that might
have shown one to the other

(for now this was a dance which
tempered the stars up through
the leaves, the green leaves) each
both thoughtful and thoughtless
toward the other, so that a
kind of wild stare was needed.
Without that stare each could
disappear (or was it entering one
another which happened?) and
a repetitive nature be revealed;
that nature, a pattern which no
longer brought itself up out of
history.

There were reflected
animations reaching out to each
in slight hesitating differential,

hands locating on the waves
of sound between themselves,
forming signs.

This told the forecast of
mood, as a part of repetitive,
historical inaccuracies. Were
they somehow tucked up or
hidden within the momentary,
knowing that moment as
unreal? If so, what was it they
were reaching toward? *Each
other?* Or the apparition of the
other within the moment?

Every grain of sand upon the
nearing shore still sounded

and hemmed the little copse, susurrating, bringing in the *real* world. It was not the usual world any longer but an appendage to the garden's rapid growth, an ocean of encompassing hint and glint.

Is it true that once the eyes have seen they are never again biologically capable of forgetting? If so that might explain why the nearing shore (with its sounds, its quaking) and the garden seemed to be occupying *one* space: a largess arc that was neither above nor below.

The doubling pair (who even though they were separate, could also identify *in* unison) stood up from the ground (where they had lain) after deciding that to be abrupt, to instigate face-off with the earth, was just not graceful. Much better to engage a pose that would allow stare to flourish, they thought. Much better to not offend green.

They walked in a tip-toe

fashion, gently whispering phonemes. Not whispering of or about phonemes, but whispering the little whips themselves.

The pose was such a dear sight that the birds stopped singing. Then they went right on with their own peeps and little jabs into the air. In a way these birds (descendants of the pterodactylic saurian ages) left a way into the surrounding media through their compositions.

Strange and seemingly robust clothing dropped down on each of the two in intervals: bright colored cloths made of waxwing and purpling throat warblers, titmice and cardinal.

The birds desired to know more of the doubling pair but had no way to inquire of them. They were aware of the problem of not having a shared language. They were aware of how this could impinge on their understanding of the various realms of this species that was now finally proving itself so valuable to the various inhabitants of the garden. Their poses exhibited the power to temporarily stop the singing of the birds!

Gaze began to turn

upward, met the grinning eye of one very large bird. Was this bird's eye (so vast as it was, vast enough to prove the need to change the phrase "a bird's eye view") a zone where wild horses ran? Galloping was heard somewhere out of view. Or, from within view, exactly.

They were aware that there was an infinite

supply of water in the distance. Not exactly a mirage, but a healing fund wherein the acquaintance of *to* and *fro* made its dance-step felt. A strong gust of gaze was being swallowed by the two.

Sometimes the wind would break. The partners laughed when this became a part of the score they were noting as a developing deva of devotion. Someone said hello.

Suddenly, water fell down the back, rushing into shoes. They were clacking across a wooden planked floor, tapping and clacking, spelling a spill of lovely.

Water onto wood over time makes wood

pliable. They decided
to stay dancing on the
planks until they could
actually see the wood
buckle and lift.

"Projects are meant
to be pleasurable," one
said to the other as they
shimmied and shook.

They had had their
focus inward, on the
rolling motions, for so

long (yes, in fact an era had passed) that they had not noticed the dramatic changes that began to take place in the surrounding atmosphere and environment.

To see into the distance is to form a window by which the other grows within.

The sight of both dudes made a convincing appeal to their own shapes, and by way of it, the virtue of each was revealed innately. These were the pictures, as if cabinets of wonder and heroic map, chart and even compass, filled what was only a recollection of profoundly painful void.

Deeds were being slid across the floor, each containing or offering a miracle; but these were not just any kind of miracles. These were specialized realizations and witnesses to the power of here-tofore unacknowledged human glories.

In the distance, heroic achievements were enveloped by the one reach each to each did reach. There, the doing, the window showing itself as a glassless conduit for meaning.

These were special interpreters. They could feel the rain on the smalls of their backs as well as in their palms, now upturned to the sky. Additive eyes were slowly fashioned into their life-lines and wrinkles, appearing to mutter or flutter a verbal dexterity. The eye-palms were an infinite genus, new.

  Eye-palms as genus meant that when touch of any kind occurred, trade also occurred. This meant that palm to forehead after a fall (whereby

the forehead is
knocked into
bleeding by facing,
with force, an ochre
flowerpot), would
be a seeing into a
wound.

The fact of the eye-
palm changed the
doubling dude's'
relationship to

poultice, because now, at any moment it was possible for "seeing" to be occurring, in conjunction with healing. Regardless of the human retinas being closed (regardless of the rigidness of pre-

created narratives,
the impossibility
of contemporary
closeness).

They opened to
possibility as not
only *one* locale (as
it is engagement,
previously stated as
not only one face)
but in all locales.

They were realizing
knowledge never
was the mode of any
knowing, so they
began to think it
newly by feeling.

 The sun might
have been a mere
inversion before, but
now it had no time

in which to be or
not to be.
   Sunburnt petals
fell and rose
through the gusts
of their hair and
clothes, always in a
combination of dark
and light as if the
balm were working

from the petal-
ness (as a form of
"pedaling").
  With the
impending petals
came also an
awareness of how
sunburnt petals
decay differently
than petals that

fall strictly from
bush to ground:
something about
soil swallowing up
a thing that falls
directly into it.
  This brought them
into discussions
of underworld
states, of their

presences and their relevancies.

Dissonance was a hub of their discussion about the underworlds. They were beginning to know that unlike contention in a

realm driven by
human limit,
the necessity of
their pursuit of
dissonance was a
musical one: one
with its impetuses
pointed toward
extrusions and
fusions as a way to

replace confusion.
The wood
had emitted a
radioactivity which
came and went, but
in between (down
in the under-part
of the world) a vast
library of colors
leapt about, upon

the shoulders of
sound as well as
the palms which
held their eye-
creases.

Next: to swim and
to hear the ear-
gulf which swept
along in a currency
of protean

dynamic. The
thematic note can
be recapitulated
without remorse.
Repetition never
hurt anyone.

If operations
upon the note
could be rendered
and recorded,

no doubt they would sound like this. However something always comes in to change the record.

Even though temporary positions of gestalt, bios and

the permaculture
of little etchings
could be
enciphered,
nothing held
but the intrinsic
density of these
two, their infra-
red house-boat of
shock and awe.

Their connection
and connectability
defied most
laws, actually.
Sometimes the
differentiation of
the world they
inhabited from
other laws or
enzymes shook

through them
giving them
an anatomy to
reflect upon; a
thaumaturgical
anatomy appeared
to and through
them in densities
that were always
round.

They were slinging neutrinos through excess and inferno in order to alchemically render them visible. They wanted to see, and they knew that priorities regarding seeing were not singular. In other words, they were open to seeing in different ways, more-than retinal ways.

To be open to *more-than* is to invite surplus. To invite surplus is to need to create methods for integrating that surplus into ways that nourish any current span toward a future span. These were the kinds of things they reflected on as a way to prepare for enacting. There was a place on the shore, where rose bushes abounded. One of the dudes often went to that place on the shore to reflect. When this dude

went there they
made sure they
could bind self
to those sticking
rose bushes,
figured it might
be a way to get
closer to them
through prick

and color.
  Each rounding
was not
something that
bent more than
the pose could
have wanted
in any of its
occurring modes.

An understanding
of how to see
(in the dark)
released them
not just toward
each other, but
onward toward
enacting a
paradise of forms

(the torsos!)
whose realization
would behold the
craftsmanship
of inherent
articulations (all
of them, actually).
Two had never
really fallen far

from the tree that they initially charged with and gestated within. That's why each was a mother to the other, too.

They were like

two nostrils
being breathed
into, two bunny
ears flopping
along, conceived
in the catenae
time of suns,
planets, maybe
even galaxies.

But home was where the heart always thrived, and returning there they knew they'd once again dive for joy.

The cranial apparition of

all capacities
rendered
them upward.
Meanwhile,
down below,
their infant
infinities
crawled like
little children,

little babies,
little naked
barely blood-ful
babies waiting
for the sculptor's
hand to join
them to their
spanning needs.
 They often

wondered at the waiting periods, the gestation realms. Aren't human seasons gestational realms? In other words, they were impatient. They

wanted the
gorgeous hands
of the sculptor
there, in order to
have something
to engorge on
(gods' hands).
In the state of
their waiting,

individually, they were many. So, when they were in collaborated poises, there were more than many: a multitude of

many.
Squinting,
they stared
up at the sky.
Passing the
implanted rose
bushes on that
strange beach,
they felt that

if they ever
stopped
staring there
might be an
unethical
halt in the
development
of the

elsewhere-
eyes (whose
origins were
in the creases
of their
upturned,
sweating
hands).

One dude said to the other, "dude, what if it were possible for the retinas of the hand-seams to spread?"

The other dude rejoined, "Oh yes, like a contagion."

Then dude began to look out over the fields, their terraced shapes. Knowing it was a big country, a big world, there was elation in every sense of each nerve. "This is an alternate to never!" Would the challenge be too much for them?

There was no real challenge that could threaten both of them *together*, so come to contagion or come to wildfires there would always be some underbrush or thatched area to dig into and hold out and stay to if need be.

"What happens when you die?"

"Why this question now?" the other dude asked.

"Well I was just wondering, because we need to keep going and if one of us goes kaput then that's kind of the end of all the pleasure."

The other dude pondered this and it was as if a freight train went through the collectivity of the hill country and the land shapes.

"Well, tell you what, we'll just go real slow then."

"But I was wondering about running," said the dude.

"We tried that, remember? We can only go so far before we run out of breath."

As their tread began to curve and curl around the terraced countryside, they kept to the turning aspect of the ascending and descending, very respectful of the fact that one had to conserve one's vitals for the long haul.

Eventually, they would need to invent some form other than the road in order to find the road again, as it grooved into a future. The prospect could be daunting unless they veered or swerved, discovering the natural shape and contours in the acreage of the holy bramble.

Dear dude: catch wind of my intent

Dear dude:
in that wind
we can
unconditionally
fly

Everything that is socialized as something that can be known ("knowledge") is actually a form of propaganda. The brain itself is the central disseminator of propaganda, not because of what it is, but because of what it has been engineered to believe itself to belong to. The central pressing concern of this art is to open up, everywhere and as much as possible, the view of the brain to the brain, thereby giving it heart and soul where it thinks it knows otherwise.

The thing that is really special about our engagement (here in this art) is that it issues from an event that can never be obliterated (not even by its own exuberant rush toward itself as getting up on and over itself to view what is or isn't, from any beginning or end, anywhere).

Our art is in the event itself, so embedded in it that we are the event; we are it everywhere and at all times (even when we can't write about it). In our various ways of finding the words to *say* we become one with the event in a different way, we enter it always differently, always wanting to know what it is again.

We can't ever be satisfied unless what we are engaging is a primal acquaintance (primal meaning the necessary moment of *its* issue, regardless of the category or name under which it might otherwise be able to be explained).

I don't want to explain this connection, with you or with the art. I want to bring it out as love, like there hasn't ever been love, like I just invented it or was able to invent love, to conjure it out of a potency that I cannot name, even for myself!

I want to do this by searching out the nooks and crannies, the nano-ducts whereby people might see a way in. What is this place? It's the place of permitting ourselves to understand that we are connecting up to what we really are, and that what we are never rests in the names alone.

Dreams as Artillery Enabling Till

I just had a dream with cousins saying aloud, shouting into my face, that I am not *erotic* because I am heavy. The one being the rudest and rallying folks against me was wearing a rhinestone gown and kept mistaking *the mystical* for aesthetic mirage.

I also was menstrual bleeding
in the dream and kept bleeding
onto the velvet chairs and that
excess confirmed the family's
fears that erotic was not what
I was trying to be. There was a
weird feeling of disgust in the
air.

Usually the authoring of my mouth by another is something I reserve only for my lover, but there have been times in the haunts of the dreams that my grandfather screams wildly into my mouth about the Mormon church.

This morning I woke up with menstrual blood all over the bed, between my legs.

The fire is being brought into the temple (skull in hand) as the prophetic poet's infusion: drink this heat. Do we brood for the lost mortal or do we find a way to prefer ourselves torqued into readiness over latency in the *lost*?

There are chariots and internal rhyme inside the chest. They conduct by clef. Clef sets the location, decorates the line with intent. Yet what comes when the mortal enters is assonance and dissonance, poesis *as* the active imagination.

Rhyme is bodies that identify with being banged. Bring the danger words to their own elation by way of rhythm, dear seeker. The body is where it's at: the precious value of protecting and prizing it. Body: so full of vibration and a vibration inherently rhymes with itself.

Vibration is like
sand. Sand is a pre
of soil and sand is
from the sea. Sand
is the seeker's origin
and because it is
such it can never be
abject or reject.

I eat my notebook. From my notebook to
yours now:

I have worked *so* for unconditional spring.

Done this as a way to connect to the
Dionysian strings that fuse
hostile parties
by way of the outspurts
of temporary
springs. Elongating
parturition
is and will remain
a noble act.

The doula as well as the carrier to term.

I wrote that book entirely in a trance state. I do not remember writing most of it. The trance is why it is so good.

The trance is allowing you to understand the manifold and not the singular (which is why it is working so well).

A plentiful feeling in my heart: darkness.

A nest filled with baby birds that at this moment are making no noise. Like swimming on water knowing it is *you* but of course it's water. Yes, float.

Active convergence is essential.
Convergence should be the culture but
it's not because of ownership. Ownership
is all about men and men in hierarchy.
No one can really *own land* (or women's
bodies) and that's the truth. Men tell their
male offspring that they own. Patriarchy
alienates the womb as a continued
tragedy. We must convene here: *land* is the
helpmate, the site of future convergences!

I promise to turn so much dirt that the splendor-terra of your hidden blossoms (even in seed-form) will *feel* cultivated in ways that nourish *them*. I promise to turn intents and possibilities into indelible primrose.

Adam is not the birth-sight of Eve
Eve is not Adam's birthright

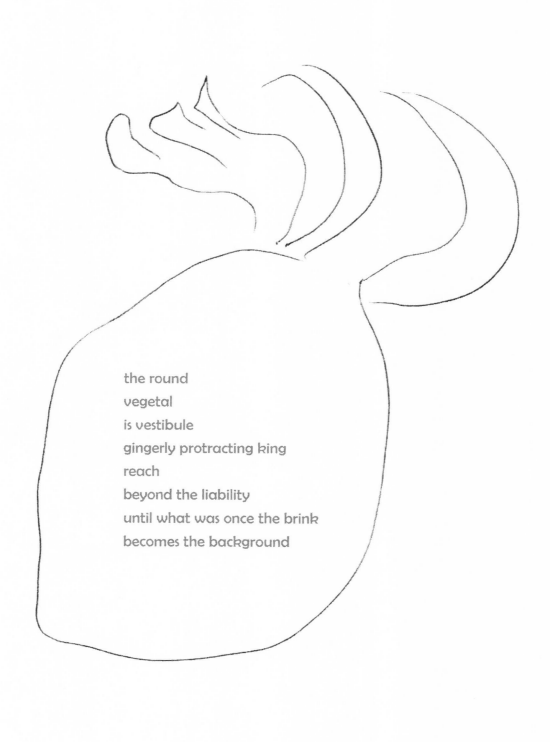

the round

vegetal

is vestibule

gingerly protracting king

reach

beyond the liability

until what was once the brink

becomes the background

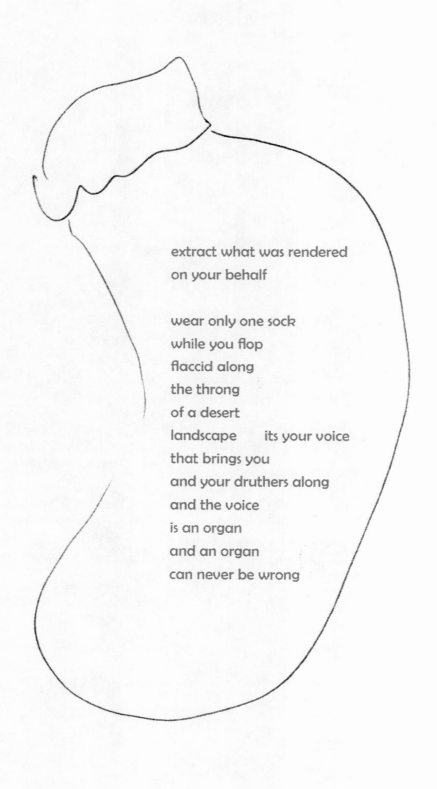

extract what was rendered
on your behalf

wear only one sock
while you flop
flaccid along
the throng
of a desert
landscape   its your voice
that brings you
and your druthers along
and the voice
is an organ
and an organ
can never be wrong

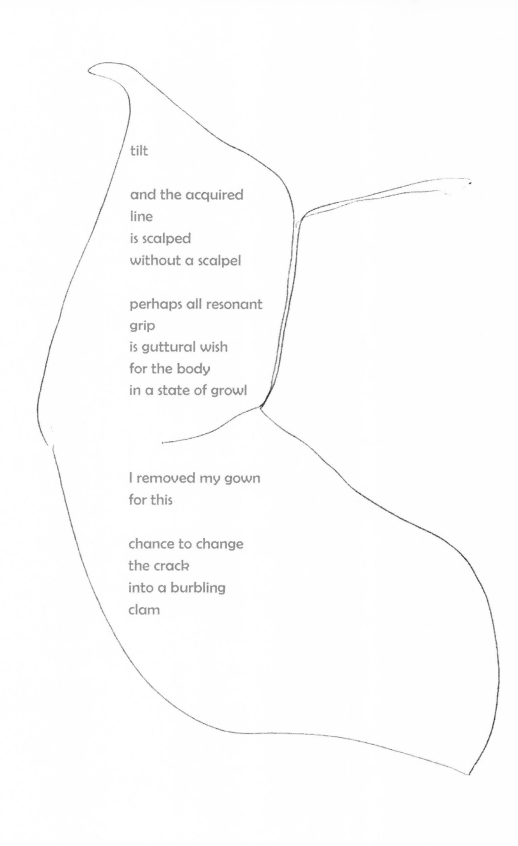

tilt

and the acquired
line
is scalped
without a scalpel

perhaps all resonant
grip
is guttural wish
for the body
in a state of growl

I removed my gown
for this

chance to change
the crack
into a burbling
clam

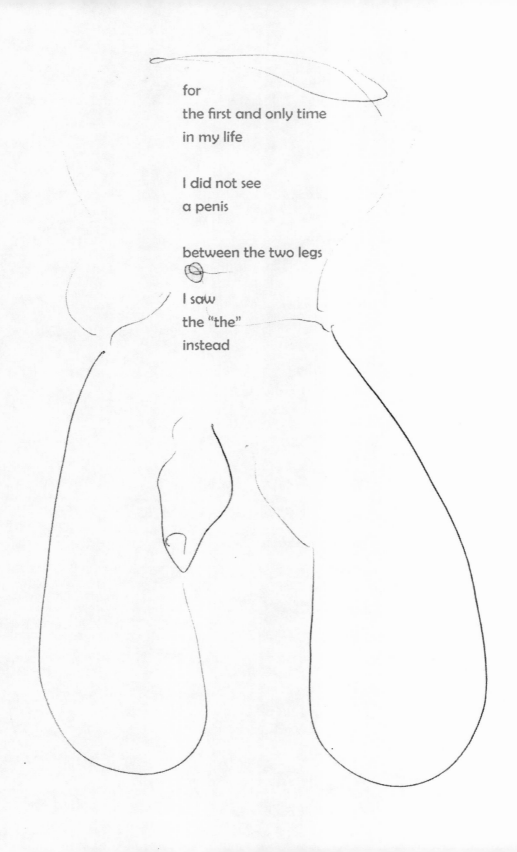

for
the first and only time
in my life

I did not see
a penis

between the two legs

I saw
the "the"
instead

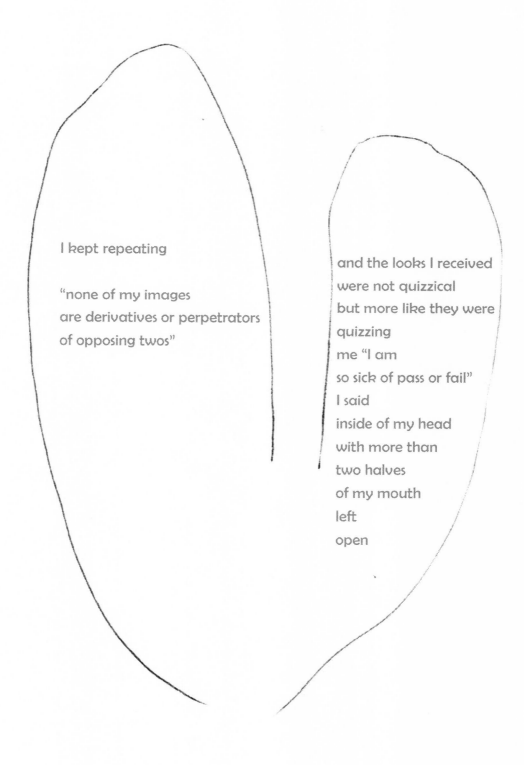

I kept repeating

"none of my images
are derivatives or perpetrators
of opposing twos"

and the looks I received
were not quizzical
but more like they were
quizzing
me "I am
so sick of pass or fail"
I said
inside of my head
with more than
two halves
of my mouth
left
open

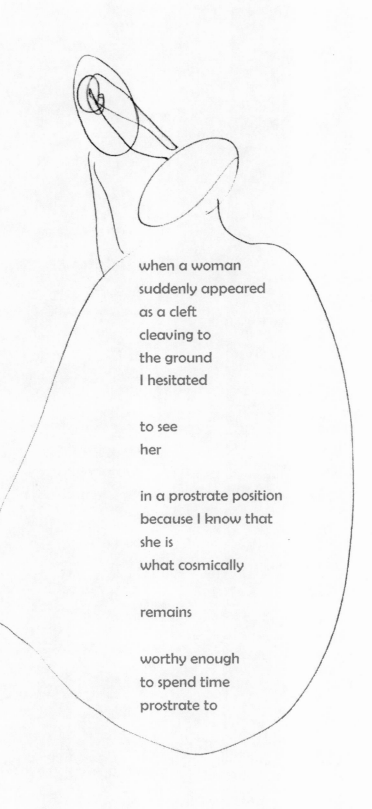

when a woman
suddenly appeared
as a cleft
cleaving to
the ground
I hesitated

to see
her

in a prostrate position
because I know that
she is
what cosmically

remains

worthy enough
to spend time
prostrate to

make your drafts
of enabling density

more deft
less daft

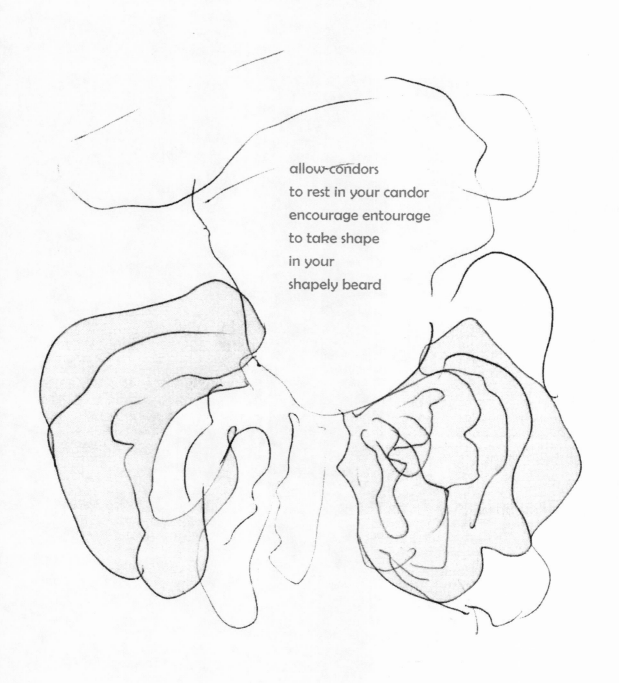

allow condors
to rest in your candor
encourage entourage
to take shape
in your
shapely beard

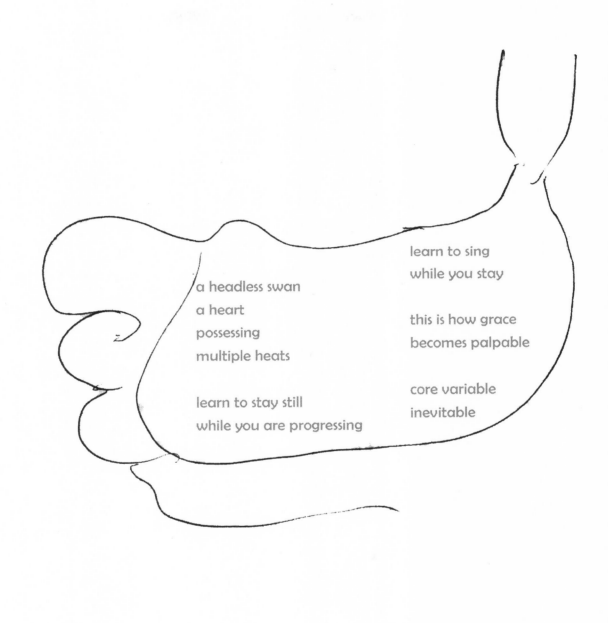

a headless swan
a heart
possessing
multiple heats

learn to stay still
while you are progressing

learn to sing
while you stay

this is how grace
becomes palpable

core variable
inevitable

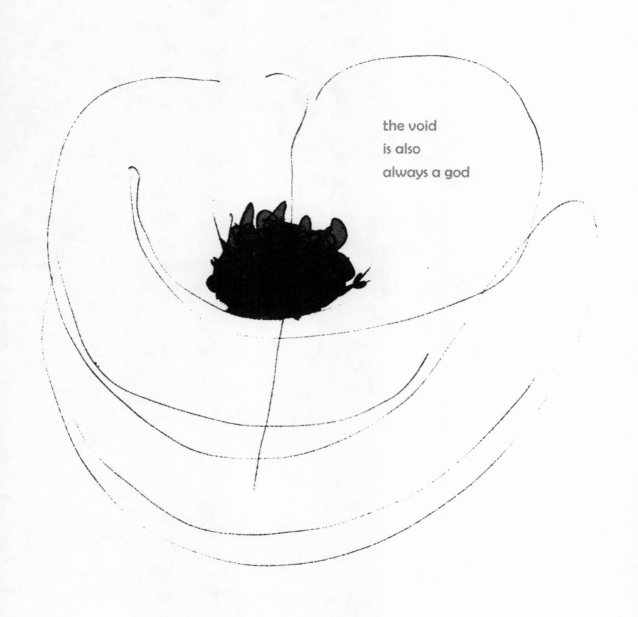

the void
is also
always a god

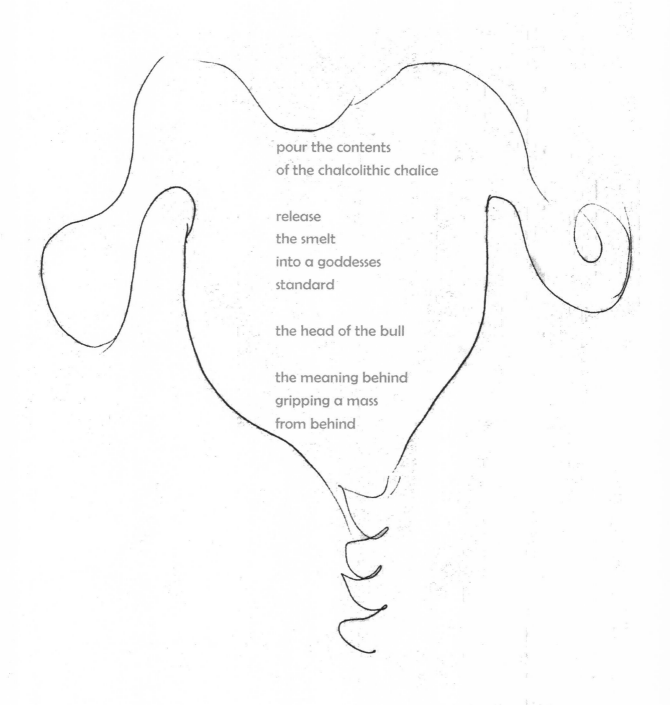

pour the contents
of the chalcolithic chalice

release
the smelt
into a goddesses
standard

the head of the bull

the meaning behind
gripping a mass
from behind

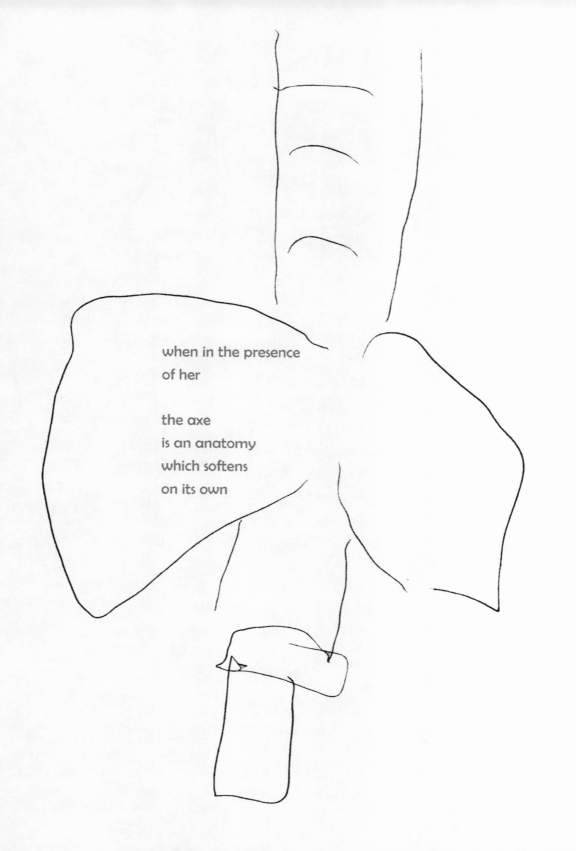

when in the presence
of her

the axe
is an anatomy
which softens
on its own

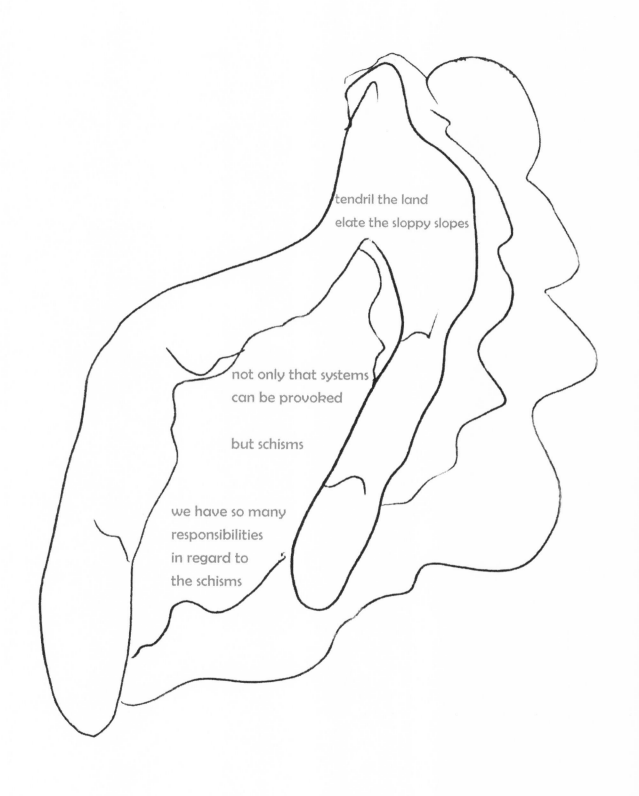

tendril the land

elate the sloppy slopes

not only that systems
can be provoked

but schisms

we have so many
responsibilities
in regard to
the schisms

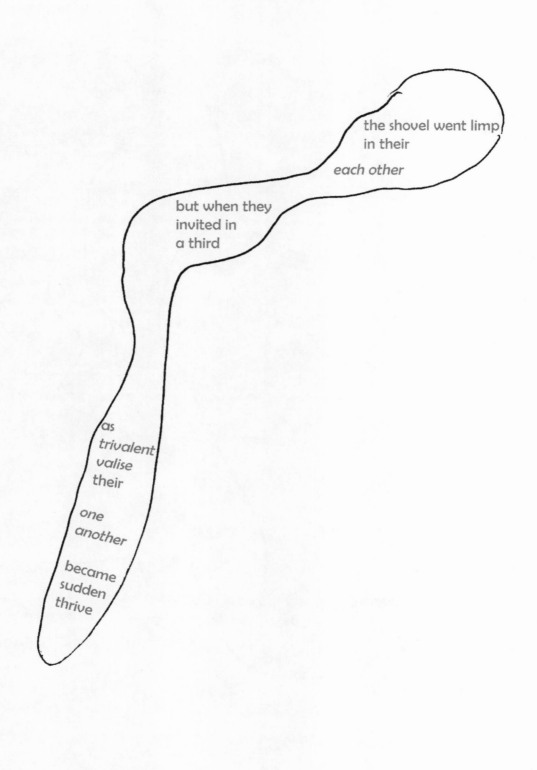

the shovel went limp
in their

each other

but when they
invited in
a third

*as
trivalent
valise
their*

*one
another*

*became
sudden
thrive*

Two Marys
are Better Than One

A Trans Novel
of Transgressive Trans-Traces

from a work in progress

j/j hastain and t thilleman

1.

CALL ME MAGDALENE. *Migdal* means fortress. I want you to assume that I am from there: that I can be your here. My town is my capacity; rest in me as I offer myself to you.

To start with Mary Magdalene we must also start with a relationship which literally cleansed the body of disambiguated genii. What aspects of one's past tenses remain within and in need of being cleansed (when we meet another)? Can our meeting, one to another, be a way in which that cleanse gets instigated?

The book of life is being written by way of a nude, curved form, dignified over the male devotees, privy to private revelations.

As witness to the direct aftermath of the resurrection of Christ, my dear love danced for me, just as I once danced for the men who paid me.

1.

IN THE IMAGE OF IMAGES, the burning bush, visions and tongues of visions rush forth. No one can see it burn. No one sees into the burning because the burning for them has stopped and it is only an appendage of their self-regard, shrinking now under the weight of their suffragette status.

This is the meaning of the mother, Mary, beheld in the little reflection cast by her across all spatial dimension. Her name was changed to *Maryam* so that she might become impregnated by the vision of all visions.

The old ways had been used up and were at an end. There is no way for man to re-enter his mother bellowing. His genitals are being thrown to the expansive sea. The spread of mankind's access to power now has to come by way of Maryam (though she rarely gets credit for it).

So it is that the *image* of the vision became mortal. The *face* which beheld the vision became spirit.

2.

As my love's most beloved disciple I presented myself as fractals in the process of being softened. I did not want to pretend. There is no use in pretending or in falsehood when dealing with the form of a cave and its contents (whether from within the cave or waiting outside of it).

Unintentional entry into beloved forms always brings forth the *radical* by breeding. Breed these distinct marvels: glandular anticipations, glutinous rites.

2.

Maryam was under the protection of one servant in the holy house, kept and sequestered, judged to be beyond belief by the judges. Belief had never seen such an unbelievable claim and indeed the very nature of Maryam as a post-lingual iteration made it impossible but to condemn her—or at least change her mind to their way of thinking.

Who would be in a position to believe her claim but this one servant? He was a servant of the highest lord in those parts. He was entrusted her, and so put her into her own room within the house in order to carry out his received orders.

Whose eyes but his were shown the abundance of food each day, as if from nowhere, appearing from her room. She ate the mysterious food, never hungry, even though the servant had brought none, and the debate went on regarding her claim; and the servant who also ate was only kept in the loop as to the meaning of these food-based miracles just enough for him to also be sequestered within the mystery, within the house.

Time ceased as she fed the image of the spirit she carried within. But who would believe him, he now a believer of Maryam's visionary source?

Certainly not the ordained nor the order that kept Maryam stuck outside the orders of life, inside the house of the Lord they served. But what were they serving if not the house as real housing, real architecture for everything the human body was birthed from and for? Were their ownerships, rights of privilege that enabled the rooms and the architecture, to remain mysteriously empty? Who was the man, if not all men, who owned the house?

The servant unlocks her door as the incense seeps.

3.

IF THERE WERE a sacred enough word for the kind of friendship he bestowed upon me I would use that term over and over again in conjunction with my obsessive pronunciation of his name. His name is really *names* to me, because I long to reflect him back to him, by nuance. Because I have not yet found a precise enough term I will instead describe: consorting with a seraph presenting itself in human form. A seraph presenting itself in human form is planning to perform itself in an unsanctioned manner: to out do by way of the cross, to inform the future by way of the blood of one's own body.

Dear friend, my master, I long to know if matter is meant for destructions of various types.

Roots are dipped in plasma, then used to color the codex: concave scrim on which to record, but more importantly than record, by which to provide abode for the sacrosanct nature of image.

3.

LOVE WAS BUT the beginning feint of a restitution for the human race. Love will return one day. Love was withdrawn from its own protection for the protection of a separation of values, and while that story explains the variousness of created things it cannot be the element which draws all things together.

Of the seven angels who created the cosmos there was one who was sheltered by Maryam. Enclosed in the vision of Maryam, a servant in the house of the Archons was shown a series of seven dreams within the image of a white egg.

In the first vision the egg rose out of waters whose steamy breath covered the entire deep and the hidden, submerged primordial. The curves of the planet and the curves of the egg were shining together even as they were different emanations.

During the second night the dream showed to the servant an egg-shaped mound which was no longer submerged in the primal. The mound of dirt interacted with the egg. Stirrings in the mud began to emit sounds. The sounds came not as syllabics but as cries which united with the prime conductivity of the air, a passage given to the pathos in all things regardless of the specificities of their differences; the cry and the following moans were all immediately incorporated through the medium of the air.

On the third night the dream bore the vision of a whirring of wings. A giant bird with brass colored and dark blue and white feathers placed the egg on top of the mound of dirt. The night sound turned to voice as a divining principle within the images it produced.

The fourth dream showed image as the protection as well as the protector of the egg itself. The air regarded the egg.

The fifth dream turned its vision of voice into the sight of the egg now covered with designs of celestial mapping. Each map dried in the air to represent a script which furthered its design. The separation of the designs one from the other began to speak. Each speech was the beginning formation of words, but these were not words that had any human language. They were something else entirely. And if they were taken to include the map, each one would inflate and create another world.

In the sixth, the pairs of sounds, with each separation of design, produced a second shell, a translucent covering for the egg. Through lucent glaze the visionary worked its design into the colors of light, further separating script from its design element, so that the screen upon which they were projected above the egg's shell now contained all silence from the primordial as well as the visionary's attentiveness and hearing.

Seventh, the membrane was stretched to the dome above until it split open. In the rushing sound of the dream a yellowish film cascaded toward the dream's shape. In that moment the dreamer knew it was belief that had helped in the emergence of all form. From the yellow and dark blue ingot of the opening of elasticized egg-mound the form and patterns of a gigantic eight-legged beetle emerged. The beetle covered the entire expanse of sky, spreading through it as if it were the primordial water of the first vision which had been entirely forgotten until now.

Out of the armor of the beetle leapt a small child who resembled both a snake as well as a frog. The child was weeping and his cries seemed to echo from every stillness and to cause rain to fall. The snake of his two natures would hide long enough to show the boy-child and its other, glinting in a spasm and flash of light from the visionary cosmos. A girl-child with a long body waved iridescently into the reflection, splattering rocks and earth in the form of multi-hued lichen.

Maryam felt the seeds sprouting under her and knew they were destined to grow through her, but this meant she had to accept what others thought of her and not try to tell them off, nor try to convince them with logic. The dream of her labor was both before and after the Logos of all philosophies and, in a sense, her pregnancy contained transcendence itself, which all worded beliefs eventually must accept as their own.

When the servant woke beside the palm tree he was beside himself; he found that he no longer was what he saw. He had become the date-palm tree itself.

4.

As a minister to my dearest friend I was inseparable from his parable. I shared many of my memories with him: how often I saw the sloughs of parabolic devils still within me (even though technically they had been removed from me via miracle), how I intentionally brewed aphrodisiacs in the lengths of my hair.

He relayed to me that my name was translated to mean curling women's hair. An implication of worth? How he wanted to see more of me? I noted that he smiled in a wry way when he spoke to me about my name. I wondered if he, speaking to me about my name, was speaking to me about my body. I admit (though I would never say it to him) that the tender qualities of his personality and his body made me feel aroused: counsel and clandestine in an instant. I wanted him to administer to me as a continuum-viaticum, perhaps in the species of the beveling of flesh: benevolent wine (which always looks to me just like rouge sweat falling from his brow) and nothing less.

As a female altar server I sneak gulps of wine while men's backs are turned to me. Should I be sharing this? I wonder if there are any revelations that truly only come to men (regardless of the norms the

4.

One vision was enough for those involved, including the councils (who could not be counted on to define even the night (their reach being neither self nor otherly inclusive)).

The councils decided Maryam was to have her little baby raised in the traditional manner, which meant she would have to fend for herself in the tribal tents. The child would have to be a servant to the rites of passage like any other. Here the separation was made as if arbitrary, and so in that guise, any and all identities flourished and took support, relying on the arbitration of the arbitrary to see their own separation (regardless of their ever-abiding inclusiveness—their humanity, in other words).

But Maryam couldn't find a suitable tent. She therefore left the oasis and wandered into the desert to give birth.

A very personal Miraj lifted her body and took her to the stone. Afterbirth spread on the stone and the little boy broke out of the sac. The Miraj took the boy in two hands and severed the umbilical from the placenta, placing him on the date palm branch next to the fruit at the base of the tree.

The little boy's eyes could see the

culture upholds)? I doubt it. Oh, probably not good to have doubt—or at least not good to say that I have it. I mean, I have some revelations of my own when men are speaking to male crowds. In those revelations, the images of men are slowly being replaced with ravenous female doyens.

sand in drifts and curves where the wind had blown. The little boy wailed; eight times he wailed until he was calm again.

The stone swallowed the Miraj and the placenta. The little boy bit Maryam's nipple as she tried to nurse and the blood mixed with her sap: a mixture of both blood and sap which names him. He would not be tamed (so he would become a definition with no proper name). He would one day rule as he did in that moment as a dark stone hovering above the lighted land. It is why he will only look for love, gathering it anywhere, regardless of the definition it was given in the past. He is, having been helped into the world by the Miraj, its ever present future.

The little boy sucked her sap until Maryam was flat and dry. Then he bit into the stone and drank from its fissure until the sun returned to its ragged, burning edges: tongues of heat that would not penetrate the birthing stone.

5.

IT IS SAID the son of god is within me, within you. What does that really mean? That my dear master, my closest friend, is not really himself? That the amorous feelings I feel for him (platonic or erotic) are really feelings I am feeling for myself? If that is the case, is intermittence the answer to how intimacy with him will always feel to me?

I am tired of overhearing Christ's male disciples ask him why he loves me more than he loves them. That is, technically, gossip, isn't it? Shouldn't such quality of speak be banned? I see it bear no good. So what if 39 of his 64 answers were in regard to my questions. Obviously, there was some value in them if he felt called to respond to them!

They just do not know about our closeness; they are unable to understand it. They know not about how behind the mound, further into the meadow, he helps me cross that shale-colored shole (the one that he has somehow lifted far off of the ground and caused to hover). We are both aware I need to work on my balance.

5.

THE STONE AND THE TREE: but the living proof of stone and tree have yet to be discovered. Separating them out for human understanding they are liable to fall into endless division which starts with the sexes and ends with sixes.

Even in the visible afterbirth the signs remained hidden. DNA revealed a script for which no tension emerged but the one. The stone had swallowed the one and told of the floor of the desert from the point of view of the mountains in the distance. Maryam was fed by the date palm tree as it rained. After the rain, Maryam noticed there was no more Miraj as nurse. She took it as sapient gesture, knowing that to make a system of its event beyond ill-advised, leads to stereotypes of all shapes and sizes. Her body was sore from this and also the realization, but it did not keep her from knowing that everything was of a oneness, that it did not come from her thinking herself a self, for instance, nor any of the circumstances of her life one over the other— her psychismic state of being was always the medium of body as well as "mind".

The councils convinced themselves that the virgin birth was a division of their own idea of power, yet the stone existed (for which they had no imagination or sight). Into the night the various constellations revolved around a cloud and Maryam was about to give her body the name of the cloud when it began to rain harder.

The little baby boy would have to live a lifetime for all the sand to wash away and the desert to be erased: one crystal being split into two halves, then the calendars being rendered useless. And any pointed finger or laughing incredulous laugh would attempt a demonstration and then a proof for the ultimate division: I and You.

Each living specter (formed under the shadow of virginity) was released and the perpetual ocularity of sound penetrated, imposing *oracular death* with the actual skin of the palm-tree.

The two-faced judgment of the councils turned against itself and inward, against each side of every judgment. Their ritualization of the virginal image became a split decision. Maryam's matter was made transcendent and symbolic by the imagination through which lifetimes of concentration within the stone, faces one of day the other of night, impregnated, birthed the boy. The boy was, therefore, the dream out of which—everything.

This *he* (and not every he) is the meaning of the visionary image: he who will enable and not disable by interpretation.

6.

FOR SO LONG it has been the usual state that women who hear voices are recluses bound for expanses of wilderness: places where we can scream at the top of our lungs and rip out our hair during the visitations. We have had to do this because in the cities we are burned in the street. "Heretical" is what they shout at us as they push us down to the ground, sandstone embedded into our knees.

When I heard them, I never considered the voices I heard anything other than the possibility that I could remain a virgin and still be a prostitute, simply because there was more than one of me inside of me. Thought to have been cleansed of the demons by my dear friend, I am not going to tell you if I ever still hear the voices. I will tell you, though, it is better to fake a miracle than to die on the threshold at the outskirts of the city.

Oh, and, if you must know where it happens and how often, Jesus regularly kisses me on my neck: right here (the chafed place between chin and breast). When he does this I think of him as a woman. I guess the complexities of that moment make us both heretical.

6.

IN THIS DESCENT from visionary event, the rule of one image became many. The little boy grew into changes noticed for the first time from the image of child to man, each leaving behind its generation the world had conjured and imagined for him.

The council blamed the virgin's transfiguration as the source for the multigenerational man and gathered together a group of policy experts to scare Maryam out from where she now enjoyed living, in a field surrounded by cows. If the udders were too full she'd pull them into a bucket and churn the half-sour milk into butter. She was regarded by others as just another man-connected body, like themselves, useless to the power-structure inherent in every field.

Even though the council had no actual authority, the policy experts still determined the best way to implement their image-based strategy for continued ownership.

The grown man was sleeping in a small room surrounded by cardinals singing in the trees outside the windows. Within each song light gained strength out of darkness and little visitations from his dreams pried open his heart as to their source. He was running between the trees with a disguised mermaid; he was running to hide only to be found by her, teased by her from behind this tree or that tree. The thighs of the dream kept parting like words in a protein bath of glistening and glinting scales around the rim of the world.

It was his neighbor's voice that always woke him so that he would not forget who he was.

7.

WHEN DUSK BEGINS to gulp the sun into darkness I play my violin at the precipice of my dear friend's always-open-door. The wound on the left side, just below my chin, often seeps liquid the texture of tarnished clarity. This wound needs to be milled.

Christ speaks to me about how our wounds are in need of our aid. When he speaks of our wounds like this, sometimes he also speaks more specifically of himself: how his ensuing wounds are cultural wounds. When he is vulnerable with me like this, it makes me feel like we are the closest of all of his apostolic relations.

Were Jesus' apostles his multiple personalities? If so, am I one of them? It would be alright with me if I were one image within his imagination. I love him that much.

The wood cutter's glands and hands swell each time they configure and re-configure warped wood into something that can be played with musical integrity. See my left hand stroke the length of the neck of this curved shape; consider the positions of my right hand and notice what the word pluck rhymes with.

"And this is how you introduce
divinity to the work, which trembles
from the act of inventing the angelic
by merging songbirds with people,
then forcing them upward until all
the trees crown."

Hugh Behm-Steinberg

Angel Bootie

and

Swagger

To loosen the literal to a dream state is the point of engagement and body. Our conversations are the angels talking. They talk the *we* as a way of stalking, coming closer too, by rocking.

It is in my nature to provide water. The clouds are *inside* prescriptions. Inside the head there are vision-clouds and they come apart and spit rain from the ghosts of ancestors who are not our own ancestors. We came to this place very late. It is going to take many roads to arrive, if ever we do. I am thinking that *if* we wander it would be the best thing we could possibly do.

My wandering might take me to you and it might not. I was thinking we only ever meet for this purpose: to wander and work something out/off.

All the recognitions are there in the sky, we just have to recognize them.

I never thought I would dream so much; more than the eye. You brought me water. No one else did. The spitting clouds weren't the only source, it turns out.

To be close
to the
ground is
a way and
a reason.
To get
in under
all those
letters
by the
glyphic
ledges.
Is there
lightning
in me?

Lightning leads the libretto. A wall of light and dark too. Mastering desire is almost not possible without a sense of wanting to be inside. There is also the approach of *safe words*. I was always interested in what I was trying to get at in all of this effort to get in.

The honey-head, the place of flood, of no boundary. Becoming enflamed with (possibly blinding) passion is a way to understand the world differently.

Hanging between: a shared caul. When the yoni is a shape and the lingam is a shape they sense each other's presence and speak; it's complex and is a zone that seems to be surrounded by many physical and psychic factors. It seems so loaded because it is so loaded.

The secret is the place of all possible permissions. A shared orgasm is a secret told.

Void is a big voice.

The body isn't something that is all
done in being understood. The body
is the floating boat, stop anvil-ing
and anchoring my magical vessel,
patriarchy! Things and people want to
nail the floating body down.

Without investing in love we won't be able to move forward. Love and the body are everything. We must take care of sick people too. Sick people *are* love and the body. Look how his hand trembles as he tries to tell you how much he loved his wife.

There has to be round and sharp
in order for a commitment to stick.
It's about wanting to get close to
your breath and your heartbeat as
what really makes you tick: mystical
intimacy.

No one wants to be a lonely angel.
I mean, that is what karma is for: to
bring us around to one another again
and again so we are not fucking alone,
hidden in the void. A specialized,
spectral community; spectral in that
you can and I want you to inhabit me
in my habit, to spread me into that.

I want to inhabit your nature (angel) and your bringing of that nature to your day to day (habits).

Angels want to give a day a heart. A heart is what can take the utmost care to see all the details without getting lost in cataloging details. Getting lost in the hair is best. We keep falling and we keep from falling: both sharp and soft.

If I fall and keep falling and have been given permission to fall then I can be forgiven all the way down as I open up the portals by feeling.

This is the necessary threading of the human and the angel. Thread is also a worm etymologically. A worm is a path. A worm is the path, bringing us to the dirt. A path shaped through the dirt. Muck can be an enabling tool.

What stays and what ages come and go?

My own body, which has this sense of being tortured, struggling. There is a memory of the making of incisions in me, lesions where the words come from or could come from.

You are talking about psychic lesions. These translate as lessons (embodiment) if they are approached with effort and ethics.

Spend your life weaving a dream catcher out of your own hands. It's about what needs to be done with what we have inherited.

Bread is visual and taste-able; it is multi. Earth is bready, infinitely fecund because it is poised as desire: the pull that matter complies with. I mean compliance like *dance* not like drudge of patriarchy or consumerism. In a nutshell: active compliance.

The Earth emits. That is why some people refer to her as the mother. Is the Earth in a constant state of empty-nest syndrome as embodiment? I wonder about resistance to emptiness and where that might come from.

Is the loss a way to maintain balance then? Loss is what brings out yearning (the heart, the urgency of the heart) and what comes as embodied result of yearning, gives yearning balance. Yearning provokes activity in the thing that is yearning, so yearning itself pulls the balance out of the yearner. Loss is a *why* re the yearning. There are other provokers too, but the sense of loss as shape, even, is the shape that makes for yearning and the I. The I is the combination of eyes, always in combo never solitary. There simply isn't a solitary I.

Do angels have "I"s? Because if angels have an I or even if they have I's that would mean that they are totally not of this human dimension but if they have eyes, then that's different. The Bible talks all about their many eyes. I wonder if their "I"s are in their own dream of themselves as images that the Earth retains (like feathers).

Is the Earth a manifestation of something? Is it the textual calling? I think of Earth as the first thing.

Are we (as propagations of Earth), then, each of us individual (made of many) eyes? And is this quantum mechanics at its basis?

Will the Earth ever forget us? Is there anything kin to sin that will move us from the Earth's many eyes?

Maybe the eyes are forgetful themselves. An Earth with no memory versus simple forgetfulness. Maybe our cells get distracted? Do the cells forget the skin?

They forget the skin all the time and are being whispered to in that time. So the point really is that the void is not the same as forgetting.

What does forgetting look like as a
form?

It is a middle.

Do middles experience sensation?

Yes.

Expression is the necessity of yearning. It's still an evolution, it's not a sequester. Parts are not isolated; parts are whole once they are perceived as holarchic. Angels are not religion. Religion in many ways is the murderer of sensation. Religions like to be literal about everything.

In place of the literal, a symbiotic fire.

What do you think the angels would say to your memories?

"Eerily familiar. You work with image as a body part. Your memories are personally confessional for me. They relieve some of my build up, some of these cysts."

I extract my cells and hand them to passersby on the street. I am ravenously doing psychic surgery on myself. It exhausts me in the best way. I am choking on my own fumes, feeling embodied and then embodying in the composition.

The circle has to be completed. A completed circle disappears from a seeker's view. Negative capability is scoring itself out. The angels are true themes in which we insert ourselves. Angels are to anathema as blessedness is to rote. Maybe they don't want to be in the damn church anymore. I would go to the places that have me on their stained glass windows, though. At least to see what all the ruckus was about.

Incise and take the beat and press it into space and time. It's about the act of singing: what the act does for the cells.

The body sweats out toxins. How beautiful the bodies would sound becoming their angelic selves. I think we are supposed to be that: the angelic selves. It is our mission to get ourselves to that place as our primal, but that has to be invented, not inherited.

Dervish in a devotion is an unconditional.

I can dull or sharpen the sword, whatever will help. They are meant to alert by sentences of light. When I went to sleep in the body of the child I woke to understand that my body is the source to everything. I understand this when I write on my own breasts: the baby bird as placement helps me understand myself as the source of a smile as light over me.

The openness accomplished in the work of inhabitation of the angel body is the oneness that Saddhus and Yogis practice for. Once I realized the miracle of the angel body I realized it was my body: that my synapses gave me all the answers. That felt to me like a revelation similar to the human breath.

It is a blessing that is a zipper; it holds the cells really tight. It is so tight that I zoomed into the elemental lesson:

chivalry with chord changes.

Bee-hive: respect for the exuberance of the cheekbone. It hurts me so that they shut down all wild nesting and the way to do that is to teach girls to perceive mechanically and not magically. Magic is where it's at, meaning non-linear, meaning hold as hope in praxis.

How can we allow it to be the case that pronouns remain confessional? Individual?

Are dicks responsible for the mis-imbuing of pronouns? Are dicks dead symbols? If we are trying to trespass patriarchal boundary must we consider dick as dead weight?

It is funny that these old names have new faces that still don't fit. This means that while we love luggage we should all shut up and listen more often.

I used to be salt driven (addicted to salt) and now I am much more pepper: deepened polyglot.

Engaging the great breath of doing and seeing at the same time, which is where the blood comes from.

You should not blood-let on your own.

Are we women together because of our blood? Yes, blood as intent in an instant. The ache is so beautiful. Blood is pure and total, tonal ache. It is not a relief.

This connects to parturition, to human offspring (which in the womb experiences ache but also the constant beloved throb of the mother's heartbeat, sent into it by inversions and round sounds). Parturition fully partaken of is god. God is covered in the blood-sense of being moved and this has a levitation about it. The blessing of birth is not the child then, but engagement of a continuum of flow.

We just need to remain able to avoid crowding ourselves out.

If the law stays in place too long it becomes historical, something capable of impinging: something that murders duende. I just saw a sign on the butcher shop, it said "burnt goat's feet for sale." It's not about any economic, it's about finding the duende and then chasing it so that it yields the worm-craft anew.

Being *underdog* is not an act it's a discovery. Or, underdog is a position that is enacted on you by exterior agenda, but to cultivate by way of it, by way of the impingement, is the ulterior. The ulterior is not out, it is *in*. *On* can be a part of *in* but it can also be part of patriarchy so we have to be careful. *On* from underneath can always be present as *in*.

What does the consciousness of a bowl constantly want? Because when you are full, *on* from *above* can be too much, but *on* from *below* is a forever support.

Investment evolves us as it involves us. What a great thing to combat all of these useless freebies.

Inhabiting in this way allows us to take our clefs onto our foreheads.

With each upliftment, we sign the seal.

You just kissed the human race.

I try to do that as often as I can.

It is a music that points angels.

Music is the difference between duende and noise.

Your prostate and my prostrate were sitting at a bar, and one P turns to the other and says: "You ever get yours caught in a zipper?"

"I like to keep mine tucked in tight."

"So that it's zippered well below the surface?"

"Not really below. More like within. But not caught within the zipper."

"Oh, inside the nuts?"

"Well, the real trick is to be able to tuck it backward, like the empty finger of a plastic glove in the wind."

"Does it need to rest?"

"Oh yes! The past lives of the penis exhaust me."

Clarity is important.
Without it you don't
know where to play.

Martyrs hold the cross up
while their dearest image
feeds itself to the birds.

Do you think phobias help us grow? Or are they deadening matter?

They must be of growth.

And anxieties too?

Psychology might have been invented to trap people in a stationary name.

A piece of the architecture is being built in in order to protect another piece. This act helps the thing self-sustain, go the distance of staying.

The gifts are
lifelong and
they replace
fidgeting.

Did you notice the boy leaning over the well? When he could have helped her out with his stick, why did he retract it and slowly form a spit wad that he dropped from above the well down into it. The moment his saliva hit the water she gave up, let herself die. She sank.

As she sank his face was beaming with light. He must have been another apocalypse boi; the story of a one-sided lode. He brings out authentic cosmic compassion from me. It's about feeling totally involved.

All compassion is stare.

Untraceable content makes me content.

My nipples are stronger than radio signals because my nipples come from the Earth. That is what they mean when the priestesses say « *dark mother* » with their heads pressed hard into the dirt.

She is dark and deep and we have to lie close to her. She is the dreamtime of Aboriginal elders. Old does not mean wise. Prostrate with sweaty head on dirt for a long time means wise: the age and the crimp.

Pudenda wings

allow internal organs to be

sexualized!

The bow is a vitamin.

When I have taken vitamins they make me feel like someone else is inside of me: mouth to mouth.

If that someone else is explained by vitamins then what is the Holy Spirit?

The holy spirit is *how* we are interpreting *how* the vitamins make us feel.

I just nearly crashed trying to avoid hitting the prairie dog that wandered its way into the middle of the warm street. I tried to avoid it, screaming "no no no," and saw it sort of frozen there. A warm freeze, soaking in the light.

The moment of waiting is waiting for the contents that are already there. The merge zone to end all merge zones is the angel's realm.

Dreams have their own trauma. That is why so many people just ignore them. Integration takes skill. The ignorance of the dream is seen in that which can be dismissed, but is also very capable.

To *trans* an image into another image furthers its life, provides nourishment to cosmic potential. Magic assists us, so does gender (if it can be unhinged from social moorings). Gender, not yet emancipated from social moroses, allows people to wear categories like clothes. That is why the magic garment is needed. That garment is like a hidden protein you can have at every meal. It is a love that is waiting for everyone: not insipidity but a real muscle.

Angel wings are the new petroglyphs and they are infinitely capable (which is what lets them be valuable to many) through many eras. All hail what aeon is doing to epoch; we ride the sun-mote into enablement in action.

Falling is the warmth and the tenderness of incubation of the eggs. It is hard but plentiful work to stroke the tonal tribe, the hip sectors. To remain an angel is to not join any dialectic (monument) but to instead invest in the shouts of a mountain.

The body is the dynamic. It has no sense of creating time and it does not need any time at all. It needs touch, not useless banter. A cosmic activism is being imbued by very real bodies. Graceful self-empowerment is the new non-government. We walk the line while we thread the line. Decay is a necessary corruption; the kind that exists in nature, not just politics.

Cultivation of joy is a must. It's not a philosophical program; it's a body flamboyancy. Are psychic forms of hygiene also forms of upliftment? Sensual nausea keeps us turned on (tuned in) day and night.

I feel like I come in so close that I can barely breathe. You are taking up space in yourself. That is the definition of wisdom.

The tongue is seeking its way in the night, into the night as an eye. Going up and down at the same time, lick the eye and keep the point of the soft tip into the pupil. This is the middle of sensuousness: the ever living water of the womb-archive always still and moving, both.

What are we to do with the
pretend science of the mirror? It
does not matter what you use as
long as it brings you vision. It is
sometimes good to stay inside,
within. The vision is with me
and I am with it. Navigating is
a breath, causing onlookers to
squint because it is about angels.
Angels are messengers.

You sense yourself as round. It is when I become world-contextual that I see myself as round. Imbue this over all portraits; I want to go in and unearth (upend) them all.

An angel's horn is the dick of a female he. A horn of plenty? A plethora?

Horns are both fast and slow. All horns are horny: the spiral and the spin. The spiral is the slow accretion up and down ladders in Jacob's dream and the dream is horny too: an unending iteration of the layers.

In regard to being touched in the middle of experience: it's fun being different selves, but it hurts to have to be the one touching yourself all the time. We can constantly learn to be a rebel through the angelic intercessory. *Intercessory* is about having somehow learned to blend seemingly opposing forces.

God is all about power and not the interpretation of power. Interpretation of power is what angels do. This is why god's dreams are fucked up. It is important to realize that your experience of experience entered me and made me leave the gods toward interpretation (which is a kind of science of feeling). There are more feelings than there are stars.

An angel that never separates from god can't be a messenger.

It is possible to remove some of the god-babble from your mouth without removing any of your godliness. The human world is wrestling with power (and losing) instead of wrestling with the angels (and becoming angels).

All experimental work is wrestling with the angel.

The
revelation
of feeling is
more feeling.

Beautiful and heartfelt replacements of the illusion of power make a single orange in a single moment matter so much! It's all in the position of the perception: that's the great mystical truth around the orange. An orange is in need of corroboration by the insides of the orange. I don't know if the external exists anymore.

Is the goddess, cumming,
our own experience of
pheromones? We must
put all of our praises
into stellar reflex. The
compound/prism identity is
a desire to get through this
world. To literally become
enlightenment by way
of merge (the union that
comes after separation) is a
zone in which we can be all
identities.

Shields and Little Purring Darwins

How to address the mythic gap?

Dear lotus sitters,

We witness many forms of violence. We are a form of violence: the slitting of the throat with the tongue of the deva lovers, clutching one another, on one foot, over the void. I have such strong resonance with these images. They are like the lovers, the sun then when they are whacked, they are the moon. I see that they are phosphor. We dream the way we do because then there is a gap. You are and are not yourself.

Never stop dreaming because if you stop you will burn the ephemeral hair bridge between this world of you and that (and there is not just two, either).

I think when you swing in it's the heaviest and dreamiest clarity central.

Hair here is ephemeral
DNA for as long as it is
attached to us. Touch
it: the pores are portals.
Portals need to have
the opportunity to
experience adaption.
Portals are people too.
Intimacy of many types
makes portals swoon.

Behind the sight is the
under-grid, a place that
could only come after
extremities of choice.
Exopanse (in literation) is
full and indelible flexure.
If it didn't flex we couldn't
evolve by way of it (think
of human muscles).

The voice being heard is twice or thrice the love but two or three more than one is still not enough. The hot breath of love allows us to extrude any school. Ritualistic gore comes from inserting hands into the hissing soil even though it is hissing, even while it is hissing. Shiva's eye is the throat of another's eye. You have to put your whole body into your third eye: unrestrained but trained.

I am a grave digger. There is too much honey to give! Open graves mourn until they are filled. A grave digger filling open graves holds them in a maternal way.

The clam is always open even when it seems closed. The slime door is not a closed door.

Let Ana Mendieta be buried. Don't be the one who pushed her over the edge. And when you succeed at letting her be buried, bring her flowers. Do *siluetas* on her decaying body like in the film *Nell*, when she puts bright yellow picked daisies over her dead Grandmother's *down there*.

Inter
view

)(

tt: Let's look at the severance of men (it doesn't have to even be a gender or genre though). The materialization can have a use. So what are the various uses of materializing? Does materialization always come as predetermination—how the material is to be used? I think not, though there are some materials that want to be used in certain ways. But once the way has been discovered and achieved, what is the achievement but the climax of the materialization? Do we have to go back to the first date, to prom night again?

j/j: So, it might be useful to consider what to do with the dick that has been cut off: with the appendage that is in need of reanimation in order for it to fit the order again, or something like that. You are talking about intuition or kinds of preference in masses (in their general sense) and what exists therein to be piqued? Yes. This is an important consideration. For me there is also the need to continually examine how the piquing is taking place: from what position we are reaching. That, to me (like holding up the violin a little higher than usual in the concerto or walking with exuberant chest because the sun is tucked behind a cloud), is where relationship becomes capable of deeper amplification. Let's just agree to never forget the prom night, to treat our reaches (our loves) with the awarenesses we acquired on that first night when we went a little too fast, and we hurt her for some unintended long term. Let's move slowly and entirely with honor so that we are sure whatever it is that we are touching is not being imposed upon (while we are shaping its pose toward poise).

tt: You mean to take the generality and turn it into a specificity which I totally and whole-heartedly agree with. It is the specificities of this severed dick that were not seen because of the blur of the early too-fast use of it. I bring up the masses as a way to talk about the dick in that fast first use which lacked courtship, really. It lacked amplification, in other words, and was all about a tumescent activity that could not feed on amplification, could not feed on the exuberance of the chest, the instrument in the orchestra needing and surely being called upon to be held higher: higher and fuller.

j/j: Ah, *use!* Yes. Good to point in this. The point is the music, really. If you slowed down a moment more would you have been able to see that that severed dick can be used as a baton to conduct candor (as a quality of courting it *as* matter)? Clef is the designating of the location of pitches. It is setting the stage for how the music will come forth.

tt: Pitch is a resonance for finding matter. Like: what's the matter? The question in the phrase is not in the words but in the moment, so yes, we are always at the first date in that regard, and should never leave the prom. It's deviant to stay at the prom after everyone has gone home. We're the only ones left and it's a slow dance, a dance *so* slow and detailed that my feet are becoming one with the floor, like some kind of indigenous tribal ecstatic rendition. It was my feet that found the floor only after the prom was finished, when the dick was supposed to have been severed, and in fact was.

j/j: Yes. It is ok to continue on as a wallflower if that is what we were then. It can be a form of kink to project yourself as you *are* (because social norms and expectations demand that you *be* what you are *told* to be). More than anything else though, I think it is simply about not running away: about singing out with full heart (to the best of our ability) from where we truly are.

tt: There is a way to not run away and it is the place where all lines of communication jump all the tracks. But how to make that be seen in a world that clings to the severed dick and actually enforces it as severed even though its severedness is a connecting of pitch to matter?

j/j: Yes, think of patriarchy thwarted (dick broken off) as another way into the music: this time not of a man directed by a man, but a wider decree in which travel of gender and genre is immanent and aspects or derivatives are kept *near* only as long as they *nourish*. We can move like this. We can leave patriarchy in the museum and turn and turn toward the mitochondrial: that place in which we all share. It is good to be teeming with steamy stem.

Gaps remain. Why not spend ourselves in an effort to fill them with yokey love? The baton becomes a waving worm if you hold it on one side and slowly move it up and down in a glide.

tt: We are determining that this side is where we can actually see and hear the baton and the worm simultaneously. So, if I experiment by holding it up (the worm) will you see the baton? Or hear it? Or is the middle, the in-between, the place that conducts the music?

j/j: I see you most as a modern man (which gives me hope for modern America) when you hold the worm. Cradle it. I've seen enough of men, plainly, holding their own dicks. It is a thaumaturgy of sticks that floats the dock, not traditional dicks. In other words, I want to look at the colors now: what else there is. I long for the *so long* overlooked colors.

tt: It's funny how, when walking out to the end of the pier, we are surrounded by gulls that call that point sexual, or screech at the train tracks as sexuality. But there is never any effort to understand the pilings, lashed together, thick and magical timber that has nothing to do with men. And if the discussion or entrance point to the sky isn't politicized sexuality, then it is an assuagement to masculinity, as if it oozes only from one side. I happen to like my Cassandra with cowrie shell necklaces and a worm-cinched waist, coming toward my mouth so that I might worship, not what role I'm supposed to be playing but the wand's dangerous cradle, plugging with prism my mixed metaphor.

j/j: Yes, well *how* you cradle the wand is a role, right? Just not the role you have *inherited* or the role that is being forced upon you. That is really what we are trying to say: make your own way again and again. And for god/desses sake, do it in an inventive and inclusive way!

tt: The inclusion of a mixed metaphor doesn't necessarily mean you are a deviant, yet it might call upon deviance the same way the wand is called upon to be a round disk. It's not a hard and fast rule that is being followed, but something hard and fast is actually transposing itself into us. Should we lock it away forever?

j/j: Let's just instantly alter the hard and fast into something else: smoothness, more elongation. I am aware that I have a bias/preference regarding this but it is hard to fit a fat and lyrical heart into hard and fast dominances. In other words, let's pursue *legato* as a *sense of self*. That is what we could do and how we could say it: we want more *legato*, less lock!

tt: *We*, then, is the transposition of *all* positions. The smoothing of notes into one another is a way of holding up, vivifying the passages we *can* encounter and in many cases *will* encounter (they coming to fruition, coming true, because we haven't put them away from us). This raises the possibility of encounter, too, so that inventiveness itself is open, to come and go, to stay in close or wander.

j/j: That's right. There is a whole other still-quite-unexplored relation to offspring in our relationship with inventiveness. I mean, would you abandon your child in the night when they are hungry? No, you would make them macaroni and cheese and asparagus. You would be willing to be vulnerable enough to allow the inventiveness into your dreams and would be self-implored to make an ethics that allows offspring to thrive *there* before they return to another *here*.

tt: To bring something up to the surface before it has a chance to deepen/drown is just a kind of cheapening. It might mean something but all that water the lungs could have feasted on, and all the trout too, these will be felt later as losses. The packaging of the child is sick, actually, but that's what every good citizen thinks they are supposed to do with their needle and thread.

j/j: The point: let's let children eat live trout! Ok. Onward! Now will you talk to me about Clef signs?

tt: Angels have a relation to the cryptomaniacal, but they are much more interested in continuing (instead of blowing thoughts and method-shapes out of proportion or making them all the same, on the same plane). Angels understand they have to visit each and every sign and examine its sans as well as its serif.

j/j: True. They are a slow moving cult. We should also talk about kleptomanias, about how to expand the pockets so that they are capable of holding what we might pick up. As *cosmic kleptos* as long as we ask the shell, "Is it ok if I pick you up" we can pick it up. So many tidbits lead us to tons. Let's think then about shrine rooms and altars. When I was walking through the bush in Australia I only had the satchel on my back and it was full; I was a *bit by bit* kind of full/fuel.

tt: In my room of pickups I have a rear-facing mahogany chest I use for rubbings. Each rubbing enlarges toward a many-mirrored assemblage that grows toward imperviousness, a way to withstand the onslaught of violent doubt slung at me by jealous bag-manufacturers. Competition in the *shmata*-business is fierce!

j/j: What a pick me up! The main thing is that there are dynamics (once we get an ethics ironed out (or in)) aren't there? What is your favorite dynamic to rub in?

tt: There is always a hurdle that can be scissored over, much like jumping a fence. There is satisfaction in jumping, trying to clear the fence, while remaining open to knowing. I wouldn't say that knowing is something closed off for us in that moment. We have to know so that we can look at how we have been shown knowing is supposed to be on either side of the fence—and *feel* how it is or isn't so.

j/j: What a lovely conundrum. So, a favorite place to rub is the leap that gets us from this side of the fence to that. Lunge is integral, then. When I speak about lunge I am not only speaking about a one-time *umph* (to get from an increment to another increment) but, instead, I am speaking about more myopic intervals of *pressing on*. I think a most intense aspect of the work is to proceed in ways which allow us to feel ourselves proceeding as *we* most *need* to feel it. In other words, my jump need not look like your jump but you bet, as we both jump, I want to process about it. That is where true, embodied compassion (that clustery acumen) comes from.

tt: Oh! It is funny how *courting* has left the sense of the 'court' in our time. Not *court* as in a place of judgment but *court* as in a place of *courtship*, where things are given, handed over, are disbursed from. Like, there is a courtyard, and there are walls all around, but the walls are on all sides, which make my giving to you from the center of your most intense forward, a lighting-up of what might otherwise be confining. We find one another's flower and give it from itself, not from a blockage of feeling (and certainly not from an interpretation of feeling that wants to withhold its intensity—its flower—from the other).

j/j: That is exactly what I am saying. The jail cell is called a "cell" just like the cells of the body are called cells. Cells of the body can certainly not lock us out or in, so why do we perceive that a jail cell could? Clef is a resonance coming in on the air, through the bars. And look at this origami(ish) flower I just made from my spit and the bits of dust on this floor here; let's give this to the guard (you know, the one who usually beats me) when he comes in.

tt: I tell you I hate that guard so much, he has no odor whatsoever. Let's sever our ties with his world by connecting with his mustache. Then let's give him a bath in some butter and grab his shoes and hang them on our ears. If I lick your spoon it will stick to my nose. There's a warrant out for my arrest, but they'll never find me in here (amidst the wallpaper, the paint, the deep well where all wishes are granted). I want to shave you. Thank you for shaving us with your sawed-off barber-pole design.

j/j: Oh good, another opera! I know you got arrested just so you could switch one view of cell for another. It is wonderful for me that you are in here. You should have met the guy who was in here before: totally without doppelganger or surrogate-ness. He answered every question the same way every day (even with the same inflection!).

tt: Being in the most impossible position I can be in (with you) gives me the most opportunity. When I'm next to the wall then the world isn't so far away from being moved. It's not that I want to eat it and see what comes out after the eating; I really think my kind was meant to come up for air *here*.

j/j: Makes sense. It is possible to flourish and find home within internal mosses. That's what dreams are, right? I once had a dream that I knew was a *quantum memoir* playing itself out in me/through me as a way for it to be given vision/voice. In the dream I was in an alley in an urban setting: dark place, near a large metal trashcan. I was angry; I was a dude.

I punched the alley wall with all of my might and I felt the skin of my knuckles break. At the moment of that breakage there was this feeling of unintentional spread in me. Was I becoming something else? Was my mood changing my gender? What was inside of me now?

I looked to my knuckles and had to strain to make out the bright green moss beginning to form over my wounds. It was like the green was coming out of me, having gotten into me by way of this violence in a dark place, this unintentional underworld that though I was in and being alerted by, I had not created. I then realized (and the realization closed my eyes *for* me) that within that moss (if it were possible to see on a more myopic level) there was yet another dark urban scene where an angry dude was punching a stinky wall and green was miraculously springing forth as the result.

tt: You are talking about the other person that is always in the dream space. He is sometimes there as an un-knowing victim of another (or self). Part of his problem is that all of the knowledges that have taken over his internals are banging up against his innate organology. The angelic difference between the two knowledges (of the outer world or so-called facts, and the inner world of so-called feelings) is in the *banging* and *not* in either of the myths of them. His fists have turned green (another way to interpret is *through* banging a myth).

j/j: Banging your head and hands on the myth until you bleed is a good way to unknowingly breed human *and* else. I mean there we are, weeping in the urban alley thinking to ourselves "there is no place I could weep loud enough about this" as we weep. There are all kinds of proprioceptive touch going on as the moment inverts and reinvents us. All of this is happening and all the while in the moment all we can see and feel is the rhythm of our own grief. There are always things going on in a below somewhere: an underworld, or the inky utterances of your own bodily cells. And *it* happens to *us* if we just stay with the feeling long enough to not starve it, to see it through to *a next* feeling.

tt: I think what the head banging most resembles for me is the ability to *not* step backwards, but understand that a forward embrace of the human, that the fundamentality of it, is in the very patient ability to stay, yes. But it is not something that is thrust so immediate by some sort of idea of martial combat, say, but is the very source of absolute tenderness. How else can we be so elementally shocked (which is a profound necessity to our profound desires)? I am not talking about an idea of natural desires; I don't want to starve the human body just to attain oneness with an ideal.

The very place of our knowing anything intimately is entered into gingerly yet firmly, surely, confidently, until a full immersion is possible. Shock will occur no matter at what rate the plunge is acquired because it is shocking to be fully immersed, like taking the voice out of its voice-box and playing it through a series of un-mortared bricks: the synthesized mortar will only be achieved and applied by sweat and the space opened up by stamina. It's the size of stamina that becomes the matter needed to complete the full-throated song.

j/j: Oh yes, you are talking about the tone of the stay. This is not martial combat; it is not desperation or fear-based flailing but an attempt at wisdom in stay. Isn't wisdom in stay (inclusive of widdershins) the type of an awareness a planet might need to have? We are trying to not waste the materiality of us; we are trying to have our materiality be of worth.

Now your talk of shock is really important. It is eyes filling with red when the full body immersion of a baptism is taking place. Do you keep your eyes open as you go into the sear? If you do, do you become a progressed seer by way of that?

tt: I think the emphasis on tenderness is really not a way to be methodical, but to temper the way one becomes a seer. There is a sense of going into battle, and one has to be ready. But it is not a berserker mode, like a warp spasm thing, it is a very controlled trance, one that comes from really knowing and desiring a loved one. You have to keep your eyes open in the salt-water to receive the dream. In my dream-shape the conch woman came to me to elucidate not just the psychic parts of *me* but the parts of what it means to be a *part*.

j/j: The conch woman is a hope for me; she spasms the revelations *in* by way of an elucidating darkness (as dream is). I like my revelations coming to me prior to my asking for them. I like the cornucopia splitting open over me. I like metal likenesses to honeycombs to drip over me after I get out of the shower. This way, what I have to focus on and refine is *integration*, my prostrate bow to the information that comes in and my simultaneously non-cliché self-love which allows me to know *I am worth* all of this mystery.

tt: If it weren't for dream, we'd have no way to access our evolutionary dynamism. Instead, we'd become the victims of our own outrageous laws. Every dream gives life to the dreamer, moving past boundaries, transgressing everything that is sacred and profane for that one glimpse of the worth, the value of our embodied mystery. Without that mystery visiting us and overcoming us, we'd never be able to speak, and if we couldn't speak, we'd have no way to evolve. Writing is a speaking out through the angelic delivery of our cosmic shapes; it is a place where we get to catch the cries of our ecstatic (and very difficult to know) selves.

j/j: I want to catch your (a you's) cries. I want to catch my cries. I want to be a place where both can entangle. Is the lack of this (a caul-like, infinitely holding and enabling shape) in materiality why so many of us spend *ourselves* harnessing or belittling our desires? Because there is no public place for them to reside?

tt: Oh, I think that's a very important point: we are constantly being isolated from ourselves and our nurtures and natures and yet we think we are progressing!

j/j: So as always I want to go to enabling activations: how can we guarantee ourselves that we will keep ourselves in proximity to our natures in ways that honor them? And do we have *many* natures? How to navigate those? I mean, we have to have what the Christians refer to as "the mighty change of heart"—that abrupt, that permanent. But where is the change occurring actually? I think the change happens in our desire.

tt: It is again morality (very heavy) which wants to check and strike against desire, any desire. It doesn't want desire to come into the moral. Wrong! There isn't any moral without desire, exercised to its fullest. How can anything be known without desire? Cultivating desire spreads it out and doesn't ghettoize it.

j/j: Yes. If we can conceive of desire as the toggle that balances out components of mystery then curiosities (and experimental applications) in regard to what is or is not moral can have a space. How else would we hope to deduce (accurately, with even a semblance of wisdom) foam from foam? Desire is foam; what is or is not moral is foam. Let's load our spoons with these inquiries. Let's reject any possibility of psychic or spiritual famine for the sake of what we might find in feasting.

tt: And I get that! I mean, it is that we have to be over-saturated by the forest of this world. Otherwise, if we aren't over-saturated, we are holding back from finding the real answers. Our bodies are an answer, and the shapes they have are akin to these physical presences and their beingness in our lives; they aren't merely images or allusions, (of course not!), they are the dream that gave us the angelic egg, the body by which we were given a chance to birth our own personal revelation into the cosmic. In other words, we are not from a group as if that group has a control over the sources to our signs. It is all us, our bodies, in an elemental position to one another.

j/j: Yes! And to take that further, possibly lending it toward an ethics, we can see that even the unfertilized eggs are of worth. Maybe we do not have near enough methods (for interacting), and frameworks (ways to interact) to allow us contact with the myriad potentials. **I mean think of it: the wealth in one cell! And how do we share that? Is there a writing form that exists and is currently able to hold the spilling data of a cell's telling?**

tt: If the barnyard is the goal, all fenced in and leading itself to slaughter, then why do we even have eyes to see? It's a simple question: I saw the birth of myself in the light (because of the baby bird that you were holding in hand, intent to bless it for the ritual). I saw you smiling and knew your angelic form in my crossing toward, to greet there at the birthplace, the deathbed.

But guess what!? In that instant, I was totally made one with my own body by way of a depiction of the bio-reflection in our friendship. I see this kind of friendship as the emergence of all cell-life, whether fed toward bio reproduction or not. It is the shape of the wonder of being alive.

j/j: Crossing with *animating intent* does make us in union with our own bodies! That is the marvel of it. It is like considering an egg in the context of its sides, before the egg has even been broken. From what vivid well do the angel wings protrude? From the centers of previously thought-to-be-impossible eggs! In other words, perhaps the farm itself is not too bad a place as long as what goes on therein is kept abruptly in air, materializing many forms of energy: some of us are breeders (in the 'have and make a lot of human babies' sense) and some of us breed new emotio-spiritual species.

tt: Attaching oneself to the sides of the breeder-scene is really something that I think shows a tenacity for value beyond the ordinary. It can only enliven the rest of the breeder culture, and that's what is so very important in the same way cross-genre doing and thinking contributes to mainstream desires.

j/j: Interesting! Then it looks like between the two of us we *lick the platter clean* because I am *all* about ulteriority and development of seemingly far-off or abject locations where beings deemed abject (or who sense ourselves as abject) no longer have to see ourselves in that way (in opposition to someone else (due to how we have been termed or assigned)). In other words, there will always have been an undiscovered and not-yet-inhabited cave. We can trek and trek until we find it. All that is required of us is drive, self-sustenance, persistence and patience. Who says we have to live in a suburb if we don't want to? Who says we have to have our trip with our lover on that day, when the lake is half frozen, in an actual boat? There is always the possibility of building the architecture you most need surrounding you, now.

tt: The idea of culture is that the cultivating comes from raw resource, right? It doesn't come entirely from what has already been cultivated. How much finer love and desire can be, and how much art can contribute to that understanding, this age has only begun to catch a whiff of.

j/j: Oh yes. And the illusion that it has all already been done before is total bullshit. I mean, if I moan right now, from a true and authentic place within me, has that already been done (just because someone somewhere else is also moaning (possibly less authentically) as their husband (?) is fucking them)? I think not.

tt: I would add that what validates some things (culturally speaking) is in that stuck metaphoric husband-wife-fucking mode as well. It is a way to capture moans. Lots could be done if the moan were written about in a way that didn't always assume it's already been perfected. But this desire to reach a needed authenticity resides in the sense that an infinite number of possibilities for relationships to moan haven't even begun to be touched upon.

j/j: Ah yes. And who wants to capture something *so* of the body that if let loose, if enabled to remain feral, is capable of being the path to a personal enlightenment? I mean, that is like cutting your own *integral*. I don't ever want to have been in any way responsible for having made the moan wilt.

Let's go a bit deeper into conceiving of the moan (and relationship *to/ with* the moan) as we would conceive of an asana. The work is simultaneously to find the heat at the heart of the pose and to treat the instant of embodying the pose as one would treat a very private or personal relationship to vivifying prayer.

tt: I think that of all that gets overlooked in art it is the deviance that is inherent in it. I'd love for the art to always find a deviant path into what it enjoys as a way to build the vocabulary (and not just look to words or colors and pigment as building blocks to a big ol' block of a block). This moan in me is meant not just to be isolated and perfected as a fashioned object; it's meant for you to wear, to express *swagger* in.

j/j: Thanks for using one of my favorite words in the world: swagger. In order for the art to find a deviant path do we not need to bust the locks on our neural ducts, make them flexible again like they were at birth? Do we not have a responsibility to arts' potential to open space for them? And can we intensify our own evolution by letting our bodies open to being locations of that space?

tt: You are talking about the art of never letting a discursive thing come to a halt and then be defined as it is swallowed. I'll swallow lots of things, but that's because I have to eat and I live by the mouth, just like everyone, but my humanity is not just in that as a mechanical and rusty rote maneuver. We can test everything; we can imbue the art we are practicing by penetrating it with our full-on presence. At the same time, that's not one entire era or age. It is about a two-stepping, a dance where both the partners are *in* the dance.

j/j: Yes! And all too often we overlook our partner (when it looks to us like our own face) because we fear being haunted by them. You live by the mouth; that makes sense in regard to what I sense in your writing: the large swoops. I believe that the mouth field gives off an electromagnetic radiance (like the heart field does). We can talk to our partner as we dance with them. We can show them that we are willing to *collaborate* Rumi's shared field.

2.◆

tt: When I was young I thought older women were attractive, but in a way that was much different than any other attraction might have appeared in range, so to speak, closer to my own age. Now that I am older I still have an attraction but it's so much deeper, and it also goes toward an appreciation of younger, too, in a similar way. It's as if we are on this arc that is kind of tortuous, the attraction like an attraction to a very sharp blade, and it keeps getting gayer and gayer. I mean, there is a lesson entering our mortal existence, driving us further along in the arc of the original attraction, higher, so that we never miss its significance, even when we're alone on the train, and reading.

j/j: By "gayer" you mean skewing, yes? The happy skew! I believe in this skew like some people believe in religion; I am invested in it, I practice it. You are right that if we pay attention our own authenticity and the perpetuity of moving matter brings us into an ever renewing arousal in regard to_____. Aren't we lucky to have such access to things that might increase our view? Deepen our ability to feel (which in turn deepens our skew)? I guess what I want to point to here is that perhaps there is no "original" attraction at all, but instead the skew is sort of forever growing, gaining a livelihood through *us*. In that case skew, is its own psychic species.

tt: I think of all those rivers and how they used to be so teeming with Salmon. No wonder there is a god there, and gods; *gods* are pretty. The ultimate arousal and attraction is the teeming, which is not just one flounce of water or hair but the whole seasonal river run. There are other animal signs that we fall under too and by which we understand we really are attracted to the length of beauty, the depth of the "skew" you are speaking of, the blade cutting into the moving sense of living matter we as humans would otherwise kill.

Why kill? Because we are a screwed up animal, that's why. The dream (and it isn't even just the dream) says we have to see according to the clock of the text and the law in an x, y and z gridded fashion. Fine, we can go to the moon. Fine, we can travel at light speed. Fine, we can work at a cure for cancer. All of these are wondrous but they come out of a stage and never a teeming, never an abundant show of all that is wisdom in order to shine from what they are also categorically *not*.

You don't present yourself because you are human. You present yourself because you are involved in an art that is ongoing, that lays itself out on the sticks to dry in the sun for trail jerky, for chewing, for cellular exchange.

j/j: The teeming is in the species, too. I mean you don't have to go outside of yourself in order to be a *part of* (which is the illusion that Patriarchy and Consumerism work together to attempt to convince us of). The Salmon are inside of your sexual organs, so are the titillating eggs, so are the images and the DNA memory of a chicken barking, a cloak sweating.

When we talk about moving in flow or with flow, we are speaking to the possibility of enjoining disparate atoms within our own forms. We can be the cause of acumen, of unexpected congealing. Nothing is far off from us. We are *in* matter which means we can serve matter; we can serve by swerve.

tt: I like that you say we can, we have the ability, to serve matter by taking stock of an inner. We are cultivating our intentions and we are thus not *just* dispersing them willy-nilly, like gun-fire. To extend from the cultivated inner is to stay within and then seek to hear the answer already available to us. But what was the question? What took us out of ourselves and made us into hyper-rational functionaries for our own extinction?

j/j: Not just taking stock or buying stocks, but planting stalks *within*! We are on the precipice of spring here and it is possible to move forward with effort to help those little buzzing seeds vibrate harder, more. That is a living definition for passion, isn't it? The availability of the answer is as sweet (don't you remember the cream leaking from the stalk tips last year) as the answer ever was.

The hyper-rationale that we have become as a State needs desperately to be brought back into the body. Do you have a weeping seed in your hand? Return it to the ground. Give it a chance at sate and slake.

tt: Every time I climb back up the mountain it gives me the shape of what desire had made! Lying back and thinking that all life should be molded to the desire *for a lie* (in other words, for the clothing of all ambition as a sanitized sacredness) curses the seeds. We have the literal version of that in Monsanto now, of course, but it is borne out by the ability to deny that the past has anything sweet in it!

Ripening for a future pretense is a pathetic fallacy. The phallic in fallacy is effort to deny nocturnal emission, to pray for the light of its own sun to replace the light of the real sun. There are energetic fires from the real sun in the real seeds of my own memories. I cherish them as life-giving, not as something to be put away and buried. I have to work for getting to heaven. Why would I rest and refuse to climb? Don't I have a duty to make love equal to its universality? Isn't my desire found in what was the most satisfying practice?

I think there is a fundamental disconnect to all morals because of this sense of seed-satisfaction, and it is not just part of belief systems, it is in the fundamental relationship to light and air. The *beautiful* is on the rooftop of the world.

j/j: There are whirling burls, teams of joyful gnarls. Let's all of us (in one way or another) make our way to the land-based opportunities that we are. Might this require (enable) a need to lie back on the back (that vulnerable yoga position: *Savasana*) actively? Might it require that we eat poisonous berries? Drink from the seemingly clear cascade only to find that what we have taken in has somehow been tainted by someone else? Porcupine's poop at the base of the pines; the first time the pines turn it into dirt it probably tastes a little funny to them, but over time they adapt. Vulnerabilities can help us adapt!

tt: You remind me (regarding porcupine poop) that the way to develop anything is not to have the thematic be the only guide, nor the way into the music become the *only way* it should be played. You have to breathe and that breath and your instrument are part (in fact they are the part that is the whole of the resonance of the piece) of the art object. In every making there is this very vulnerable and timorous acquisition from the first.

j/j: Well right, unless the thematic is *multi* (prong inclusive), but that rarely is the case and it certainly is not what we are generally socialized to enact or feel. How beautiful to think of breathing itself as instrument, as primal urgency that we bring to instrument. So really, we are relation making more relations. Quite infinite, aren't we? From here, do we not need then to approach, continuing with our hearts, minds and efforts poised toward *renovation* of what we are in fact socialized with? I for one am not fooled by the limit of an imposition.

tt: Limits may be just the moment of the fullest realization *as* illusion. And illusion is something that is primarily screen-based and holographic, whereas we want to deal with the resonances and how they cannot be disorganized by a mere new screen. We want to be able to continually toggle the great big node.

j/j: Yes! There are so many great, growling, hairy nodes in the outstretched wings of angels. They eat our moans, our resonances; they depend on our outbreaths and the little grunts we make as we strain to hold the pose. **I think one of the most wonderful things about the everlasting node is what a firm ship it is.** The other day after priest/ess temple work I laid on my back in the gently falling snow and watched the roof of the temple protrude like the helm of a ship.

tt: The old sense that images are stronger than the symbols we purport to cultivate comes from this holding of the vision of our humanity in regard to the node of both seeing the big and the hairy as well as accepting it as a magic wand and as not just an intellectualized presence. I think it shows on people's faces (particularly men's faces): you can see how they haven't had any chance to open up (not just to smile, but to relax into an open levitating engagement with themselves).

j/j: Sweet men: patriarchal lineage who though they perpetuate patriarchy are also so damaged by it.

My Grandpa used to always say (in regard to the grimace) "If you hold your face that way for too long it is going to stay that way." Picture him with his missing teeth, his face not only in a grin (admitting the gaps in his own mouth and body) but further, into a mime-like constancy of awe and strange glee. Now, he might have unintentionally arrived at expressive release of Kundalini in his spine, causing him to be a bit of a trippy-swirls kind of person, but *gods* did I prefer that over the calcified, arid and hard lines of mens' usual faces. Pondering my sweet (often called "crazy" Grandfather) I think that emancipating things probably begin to happen (in the body) when you hold your *whole form* in a *grin* all the time!

tt: There is this sense of authority and then security that everyone, no matter their gender or species tends to oscillate around and that is something that when putting pen to paper or finger to keypad changes the fundamental relationship to language. This is why people think that language itself is the constitution of a game. But that doesn't make sense because if it is the game being played then there would be winners and losers constituted by *it* alone. It is power and the different socializations that ensue from it which organize a game in which there do exist winners and losers, and language is only one of the weapons or tools used.
But what about feeling and sensation? The entrance of feeling into the associative patterns of the poem calls forth an internal register by which individuals enter into correspondence. This is a happy coordination and one that resists the academization of relatedness: a happy and joy-based relatedness which folds us into one another as non-fortressed, yet strong and elementally centered.

j/j: Oh hallelujah! Yes, what about feelings and sensations? I mean I could spend all day in every life pondering that by myself and with others: making bridges out of the gusty *gists*. I guess it all always returns (for me) to the hybridity and the multiplicity of angels' wings. In order to pursue wings which are not built off of *terminus*, which are not just here as space-holders until the bearers of them die (like the wings of birds are), there must be pursuit by ethical path to the elemental eternal. **When I say elemental eternal I don't mean a flighty idea only, but a weighty one: one very much *of* Earth (while it is also paradoxical palindrome for Earth). I am hoping for a never ending way to fold eternal pain into something livable in an everlasting.**

tt: You raise it all when mentioning an ethical pairing for feeling. It's why we are stuck in an aesthetic limbo, a false dialectic, when we perceive this lack of ethics in regard to feeling and writing. Instead of an approach to the ethical eternal we have false projections of power, whether they are an adherence to acceptable prize winning writing and art, or are a reaction against the purposely bad, there is really only the projection of U.S. power and not any approach to the cultivation of feeling within an eternal.

We have patterning based on private, secret conceptions and stultified public frames. Cultural products are usually projections of a political flirtation, a social rendition of form instead of a near, up close investment *in* form. But this is also another legacy of western industrialized aesthetics. Sure, we can study the 100 year arc of *objet d'art* movements and defining statements and their outcomes, but most of that arc came out of a projection of power which had only faint traces of that one-way bias. I mean, it's all there in any simple study of the arc of industry and factory culture in general. But what about the similarities, say, between the psychological embodiment in non-idealized magic spells from 2000 years ago and their psychic equivalent within a stand of wild lilac outside my therapist's window. The smell is powerful and extremely motivational!

3.

j/j: Are you ever disappointed by your dreams?

tt: Yes, when they are very concocted (which happens), but when they are startling then I know they came from a deep place and it might be a silly place too!

j/j: The concocted is often the familiar (at least for me) like have I felt this before? Ah man, I was hoping to feel something different or to feel *this thing* differently (in this context I would even get tired of redemption or glory (two great subjects/sensations for me) if I had felt it too many times in *that* way before).

tt: That's precisely the moment that happened in the creation of psychic measurements (and that includes psychology) because it was a moment of understanding that the phenomenon of creating civil places concocted and familiar was getting way too easy.

j/j: I agree! I guess the real point here is the recognition that authenticities are never easy; there is always more there to be engaged, to be entered. Turn Jacob's (eternal) Ladder upside down and climb into the crops.

tt: I am thinking about the way the tower, what gets built, also gets blasted, so that it be a centeredness between the eye and the mouth. There is a difference (slight) in the idea of eternal and the idea or sense of infinity, I mean.

j/j: Oh yes. Eternity is a hearth in the middle of feeling (that goes on for duration). Eternity is a new type of time. Infinity, however, is the way I was talking with a friend the other day about my own personal afterlife or my non-body ecstasy (post-death) and how for me it would consist of me understanding myself as an *immeasurable vast* that others are engaging themselves within or by way of. In other words, infinity has a limitless density. Eternity is a limitless time.

tt: Investing in *oneself* as *limitless* turns all the tables into their legs. We must walk around this earth as not just an ideal but a very real engagement with the false mask of people (all people including one's self) in order to get to the deeper connections that are being made. The dream space only slightly records this, or is a part of it as a beginning of the deepening into the elements. And when I say dream I mean that science and math (and all hard and rational things *are* also dreams too), partake of their nature in a dream space also.

j/j: Very true! And it is not always clear how to have "real engagements."

There is no unconditional framework for authenticity but there are many frameworks modeling falsehood. I guess a good way to proceed, then, is by demand of one's own emotions and sensations. If we approach our experiences indelibly unified with our intent to never falsify our emotions and sensations, though we may be the one throwing teacups into the street when we find out our lover has cheated on us, we also are not the ones who unintentionally retained old songs or old images as latencies to pull us down later. I guess I am saying I would always rather be the girth (even if socially unacceptable) of a now, than to store fragments of my emotions and sensations in me in ways that might enable them to trouble me later. I believe that space is vast and flexible enough to hold the viscosity of *my now*.

tt: This now that can also be a *you*: a way of putting yourself wholly forward very knowingly. Why do we have to constantly use the same words, for instance, to evoke procreation/sexual congress, etc. It seems as if we, as a culture, have absolutely no idea what procreation really is, what it means to be *pro-creative*! Can I leave my shoes at the door or do I always have to muddy the primal form of my awareness in order to graduate to my unborn self? Why must fruition and coition be forever unborn? There might be some latent truth in that but there certainly isn't an understanding of cycles that go beyond ideation. Instead, there is a constant push to penetrate transcendence as an omni-answer even though it might remain unborn and unfulfilled. This is a disaster! It is not only an inauthentic response to creation but it actually makes useless mental clutter—and clutter isn't clarity.

j/j: A couple of thoughts here: please always leave your muddy shoes in my lap: I want to integrate others' murk by strange ingestions. It is ok with me if you stain my favorite cloth. Now, on procreation: you are right, there is so much more out there (in here) than the general picture in regard to child-bearing.

Don't get me wrong, if you passionately want children and are capable of caring for them, then that is definitely part of the picture, but it is not the only part. We can procreate next versions of *ourselves* (unborn self into formed, birthed self) and *doula* them into fruition. I believe it is totally appropriate and necessary to generate forms as bridges: new self-segments to help us cross. Procreated offspring can procreate us again and again each time we imagine. That fact gives me hope!

tt: Oh the beauty of being able to be seen and to see! The endless assertions of self into another living creature (that one would call son or daughter) is nowhere approachable as an art, but is part of a State-craft. Those crafts are not reflections nor illuminations then, but are part of an obligatory campaign of laws and the interpretation of law and an obedience or disobedience to the law of the State. In the formation of a psyche that would assert itself into our art, our poetry and our writing, *we need to be able to see with our own eyes.* In this way, we become the eyes of all those families then without prejudice, and this is the way to realize moments of birth and death beyond the State, beyond the limited eyes of the State.

So our procreation, then, is multiple and manifold and told from the point of view of the entire persona and the elements involved in that act and in that family-rearing portrait. We can see the whole picture and turn it around and over and penetrate it and vivisect it with our art. We can see it. I have multitudes swimming in me, I know, and this is why sometimes in our collaborative path, I have a pregnancy that a male of our tribe normally wouldn't go through. **I bear it to its term and when I can't understand it, you help me see it (me) by the light of others. This psychic laying onto one another of living and biological realities is part then of** what our psychologies would otherwise have over-looked within the quotidian.

j/j: Ah yes, the continual self-initiation of teaching oneself to see with our own eyes; this is difficult work. How to tell the difference, if a sensory-*this* is *my* eye or *another's*? I know the traction that conveys authenticity and primality ("*this* feels like mine to me") is based in *vibration* for *me*. What is it for you? A certain picture or hue in the sky? A correlation between different senses?

The psychic pregnancy of a male can end up bearing something far more stimulating and far less normative than an unwanted child. There are reasons that the sperm that spiral within me re-combobulate my spine. It matters that they are there, compelling me from the inside out, and that is far more deserving of interest than any fear that their residence (in the erection of my heart (as opposed to a bio penis)) makes me somehow *less than* the socially/gender normative man.

tt: I would say that in terms of vibrations and hues the movement that you are referring to is a kind of extension. The fact is that we gain insight and the ability to penetrate to the quick by shunning the blab. Blab turned off results in sight's awareness of sight, which will always lead one to an array. Blab is the lie. Cultural blab is the worst, because it sends echolocations into the heart, penetrating the meat in order to flip all the switches into servitude; the blab commander who won't ever shut up!

The blab commander resembles teachers and students talking about Moby-Dick as if they really have grasped the meaning of whale blubber. And this is what informs all of them as a social movement, which they will deny on the other side of the vacuum.

j/j: This explication of the blabs that lag and make mold (not in a good way) in the blab-lab made me laugh! You are so right about the misuse of embodiment (increasing others' disembodiments?) by talking heads. I mean, what is going on with the vibrant body below the desk there, in the place that the students can't see? Far more than the talking head wants us to believe. This also makes me think of the difference between the upper "white towers of education" and the feeling you feel when you drop to your knees (getting in a trail runners way) because you see a bluebird, long dead from having lost itself in an exhaustion (due to it being caught up in a strange mesh of string tied (or caught in) a tree). One is the gap; the other is the breathing, writhing, lovely, sweaty, loss-sensed-as-meat-heart explosion body.

tt: But I also see that same form that same useless white kerfuffle of blab is also the thing which illuminates the meat explosion as well. They are meeting at the outer membranes of one another, and then eventually they merge into one another, or share one another's senses. They awaken one another to the senses and because of that they shape all other psychic reverberations, thought to be static, or even thought to be most dynamic.

j/j: Well of course it is always about the merge. I might just go to my grave blabbing about that one thing in many different ways. **I get that one thing compels another (possibly completes it, or provokes its completion) but it is also true that socio-cultural preference (and privileging one form of experience over another) takes things away from others.**

tt: I think that the ritualization of what might pass for custom, or the function of a vocabulary that gets too far into custom, works in a counter activation in order to integrate the microcosm and macrocosm within one's own place of practice. Otherwise, you have a kind of official voice speaking through your art, a kind of non-reach that masquerades.

The merge is a way to understand the fatty pleasure of existence as near-source, and when a ritual is enacted to extract that fatty pleasure, then the customary conclusions make their way to a visual plane that has been made lengthier.

My own practice ensures the poems and pages I add do not succumb to robotic speech. **But I would never eliminate the automatonomy of a cybernetic system either, and the space I clear for that system within my practice and ritualization of writing ensures that my own voice be enlarged because of that inclusion.** It's difficult to explain, however, in circles that only want your voice to play one role or another, as if to keep the different sides of metaphor as wedge lodged between your own sense of merge, your own pumping practice, your own systolic and diastolic, your own stiffness and limpness.

j/j: Post patriarchy does not necessarily mean post phallus.

S P U Y T E N   D U Y V I L

Meeting Eyes Bindery
Triton
Lithic Scatter

8TH AVENUE   Stefan Brecht

ABROAD: AN EXPATRIATE'S DIARIES   Harriet Sohmers Zwerling

A DAY AND A NIGHT AT THE BATHS   Michael Rumaker

ACTS OF LEVITATION   Laynie Browne

ALIEN MATTER   Regina Derieva

ANARCHY   Mark Scroggins

APO/CALYPSO   Gordon Osing

APPLES OF THE EARTH   Dina Elenbogen

APPROXIMATING DIAPASON   j/j hastain & t thilleman

ARC: CLEAVAGE OF GHOSTS   Noam Mor

THE ARSENIC LOBSTER   Peter Grandbois

ASHES RAIN DOWN   William Luvaas

AUNTIE VARVARA'S CLIENTS   Stelian Tanase

BALKAN ROULETTE   Drazan Gunjaca

THE BANKS OF HUNGER AND HARDSHIP   J. Hunter Patterson

BEAUTIFUL SOUL   Joshua Corey

LA BELLE DAME   Gordon Osing & Tom Carlson

BIRD ON THE WING   Juana Culhane

BLACK LACE   Barbara Henning

BLACK MOUNTAIN DAYS   Michael Rumaker

BLUEPRINTS FOR A GENOCIDE   Rob Cook

BOTH SIDES OF THE NIGER   Andrew Kaufman

BREATHING FREE   (ed.) Vyt Bakaitis

BURIAL SHIP   Nikki Stiller

BUTTERFLIES   Brane Mozetic

BUT THEY, UM   Jennie Neighbors

BY THE TIME YOU FINISH THIS BOOK YOU MIGHT BE DEAD   Aaron Zimmerman

CADENCES   j/j hastain

CAPTIVITY NARRATIVES   Richard Blevins

CELESTIAL MONSTER   Juana Culhane

CEPHALONICAL SKETCHES   t thilleman